Grilled Baby Artichokes with
Roasted Pepper Dip

Fast Pesto Focaccia

Easy Appetizers

Tuscan White Bean Crostini

2 cans (15 ounces each) white beans (such as Great Northern or cannellini), rinsed and drained
½ large red bell pepper, finely chopped *or* ⅓ cup finely chopped roasted red bell pepper
⅓ cup finely chopped onion
⅓ cup red wine vinegar
3 tablespoons chopped fresh parsley
1 tablespoon olive oil
2 cloves garlic, minced
½ teaspoon dried oregano
¼ teaspoon black pepper
18 slices French bread, about ¼ inch thick

1. Combine beans, bell pepper and onion in large bowl.

2. Whisk together vinegar, parsley, oil, garlic, oregano and black pepper in small bowl. Pour over bean mixture; toss to coat. Cover; refrigerate 2 hours or overnight.

3. Arrange bread slices in single layer on large ungreased nonstick baking sheet or broiler pan. Broil, 6 to 8 inches from heat, 30 to 45 seconds or until bread slices are lightly toasted. Cool completely.

4. Top each toasted bread slice with about 3 tablespoons bean mixture.

Makes 6 servings

Incredibly Easy
Italian

Publications International, Ltd.
Favorite Brand Name Recipes at www.fbnr.com

Pictured on the front cover: Baked Risotto with Asparagus, Spinach and Parmesan *(page 146).*

Pictured on the back cover: Rigatoni with Sausage & Beans *(page 94).*

ISBN-13: 978-1-4127-2353-4
ISBN-10: 1-4127-2353-1

Library of Congress Control Number: 2006901048

Manufactured in China.

8 7 6 5 4 3 2 1

Microwave Cooking: Microwave ovens vary in wattage. Use the cooking times as guidelines and check for doneness before adding more time.

Preparation/Cooking Times: Preparation times are based on the approximate amount of time required to assemble the recipe before cooking, baking, chilling or serving. These times include preparation steps such as measuring, chopping and mixing. The fact that some preparations and cooking can be done simultaneously is taken into account. Preparation of optional ingredients and serving suggestions is not included.

Contents

Hunt's® Easy Bruschetta

Polenta Pizzas

Skewered Antipasto

1 jar (8 ounces) SONOMA® Marinated Dried Tomatoes
1 pound (3 medium) new potatoes, cooked until tender
2 cups bite-sized vegetable pieces (such as celery, bell peppers, radishes, carrots, cucumber and green onions)
1 cup drained cooked egg tortellini and/or spinach tortellini
1 tablespoon chopped fresh chives *or* 1 teaspoon dried chives
1 tablespoon chopped fresh rosemary *or* 1 teaspoon dried rosemary

Drain oil from tomatoes into medium bowl. Place tomatoes in small bowl; set aside. Cut potatoes into 1-inch cubes. Add potatoes, vegetables, tortellini, chives and rosemary to oil in medium bowl. Stir to coat with oil; cover and marinate 1 hour at room temperature. To assemble, alternately thread tomatoes, potatoes, vegetables and tortellini onto 6-inch skewers.

Makes 12 to 14 skewers

Caponata Spread

1½ tablespoons BERTOLLI® Olive Oil
1 medium eggplant, diced (about 4 cups)
1 medium onion, chopped
1½ cups water, divided
1 envelope LIPTON® RECIPE SECRETS® Savory Herb with Garlic Soup Mix
2 tablespoons chopped fresh parsley (optional)
Salt and ground black pepper to taste
Pita chips or thinly sliced Italian or French bread

In 10-inch nonstick skillet, heat oil over medium heat and cook eggplant with onion 3 minutes. Add ½ cup water. Reduce heat to low and simmer covered 3 minutes. Stir in soup mix blended with remaining 1 cup water. Bring to a boil over high heat. Reduce heat to low and simmer uncovered, stirring occasionally, 20 minutes. Stir in parsley, salt and pepper. Serve with pita chips.

Makes about 4 cups spread

Fast Pesto Focaccia

Prep and Cook Time: 20 minutes

1 can (10 ounces) refrigerated pizza crust dough
2 tablespoons prepared pesto
4 sun-dried tomatoes (packed in oil), drained

1. Preheat oven to 425°F. Lightly grease 8-inch square baking pan. Unroll pizza dough. Fold in half; pat into pan.

2. Spread pesto evenly over dough. Chop tomatoes or snip with kitchen scissors; sprinkle over pesto. Press tomatoes into dough. Using wooden spoon handle, make indentations in dough every 2 inches.

3. Bake 10 to 12 minutes or until golden brown. Cut into 16 squares and serve warm or at room temperature. *Makes 16 servings*

BelGioioso® Gorgonzola Spread

2 cups BELGIOIOSO® Mascarpone
½ cup BELGIOIOSO® Gorgonzola
2 tablespoons chopped fresh basil
½ cup chopped walnuts
Sliced apples and pears

In small bowl, combine BelGioioso Mascarpone, BelGioioso Gorgonzola and basil. Mix to blend well. Transfer mixture to serving bowl; cover and refrigerate 2 hours. Before serving, sprinkle with walnuts and arrange sliced apples and pears around bowl. *Makes 8 servings*

Tip: This spread can also be served with fresh vegetables, crackers, Melba toast or bread.

Beefy Bruschetta

Prep Time: 5 minutes • **Cook Time:** 10 minutes

**1 loaf French or Italian bread (about 16 inches long),
   diagonally cut into 1-inch slices**
⅓ cup prepared pesto
1 cup RAGÚ® Rich & Meaty Meat Sauce, heated
1 cup shredded mozzarella cheese (about 4 ounces)

On ungreased baking sheet, arrange bread. Broil bread until golden, about 1 minute. Remove from oven. Evenly spread pesto on bread, then evenly top with Ragú Meat Sauce and sprinkle with cheese. Broil until cheese is melted.   *Makes 8 servings*

Mushroom Parmesan Crostini

1 tablespoon olive oil
1 clove garlic, finely chopped
1 cup chopped mushrooms
**1 loaf Italian or French bread (about 12 inches long),
   cut into 12 slices and toasted**
¾ cup RAGÚ® Pizza Quick® Snack Sauce
¼ cup grated Parmesan cheese
**1 tablespoon finely chopped fresh basil leaves or
   1 teaspoon dried basil leaves**

Preheat oven to 375°F. In 8-inch nonstick skillet, heat olive oil over medium heat and cook garlic 30 seconds. Add mushrooms and cook, stirring occasionally, 2 minutes or until liquid evaporates.

On baking sheet, arrange bread slices. Evenly spread Ragú Pizza Quick Snack Sauce on bread slices, then top with mushroom mixture, cheese and basil. Bake 15 minutes or until heated through.   *Makes 12 crostini*

Tip: Many varieties of mushrooms are available in supermarkets and specialty grocery stores. Shiitake, portobello and cremini mushrooms all have excellent flavor.

Grilled Baby Artichokes with Roasted Pepper Dip

Prep Time: 20 minutes • **Cook Time:** 13 minutes

18 baby artichokes* (about 1½ pounds)
½ teaspoon salt
¼ cup Frank's® RedHot® Original Cayenne Pepper Sauce
¼ cup butter or margarine, melted
   Roasted Pepper Dip (recipe follows)

*Or, substitute 2 packages (9 ounces each) frozen artichoke halves, thawed and drained. Do not microwave. Brush with Frank's® RedHot® butter mixture; grill as directed below.

1. Wash and trim tough outer leaves from artichokes. Cut ½ inch off top of artichokes, then cut in half lengthwise. Place artichoke halves, 1 cup water and salt in 3-quart microwavable bowl. Cover; microwave on HIGH 8 minutes or until just tender. Thread artichoke halves onto metal skewers.

2. Prepare grill. Combine **Frank's RedHot** Sauce and butter in small bowl. Brush mixture over artichokes. Place artichokes on grid. Grill, over hot coals, 5 minutes or until tender, turning and basting often with sauce mixture. Serve artichokes with Roasted Pepper Dip.   *Makes 6 servings*

Roasted Pepper Dip

Prep Time: 10 minutes • **Chill Time:** 30 minutes

1 jar (7 ounces) roasted red peppers, drained
1 clove garlic, chopped
¼ cup French's® Gourmayo™ Caesar Ranch Mayonnaise
2 tablespoons French's® Honey Dijon Mustard
2 tablespoons Frank's® RedHot® Original Cayenne Pepper
   Sauce
¼ teaspoon salt

1. Place roasted peppers and garlic in food processor or blender. Cover; process until very smooth.

2. Add mayonnaise, mustard, **Frank's RedHot** Sauce and salt. Process until well blended. Cover; refrigerate 30 minutes.   *Makes about 1 cup*

Polenta
Pizzas

1 teaspoon olive oil
½ cup chopped onion
¼ pound bulk mild Italian sausage
1 can (8 ounces) pizza sauce
1 roll (1 pound) prepared polenta
1 cup (4 ounces) shredded mozzarella

1. Preheat oven to 350°F. Spray 13×9-inch baking pan with nonstick cooking spray; set aside.

2. Heat olive oil in small skillet. Add onion; cook and stir over medium heat 3 minutes or until tender. Shape sausage into small rounds. Add to skillet and brown 5 minutes, turning frequently. Stir in pizza sauce; simmer 5 minutes.

3. Cut polenta roll into 16 slices; arrange in prepared pan. Spoon about 1 heaping tablespoon sausage mixture over each polenta slice. Sprinkle 1 tablespoon cheese over each slice. Bake 15 minutes or until polenta is hot and cheese is melted.   *Makes 4 to 6 servings*

*Quick Tip

Prepared polenta is wonderful to have on hand. Use it for a quick appetizer like these pizzas, or layer and bake it in a casserole with pasta sauce and shredded pizza cheese for a hearty meal in no time. Rolls of prepared polenta are usually found in the Italian section of supermarkets and are available plain or flavored (with garlic, sun-dried tomatoes, mushrooms, etc.).

Tomato Pesto Tart

Prep Time: 10 minutes • **Cook Time:** 17 to 20 minutes

1 sheet puff pastry, thawed according to package directions
   PAM® No Stick Cooking Spray
½ cup prepared pesto
1 cup (4 ounces) shredded mozzarella cheese, divided
1 can (14.5 ounces) HUNT'S® Whole Tomatoes, sliced

UNFOLD puff pastry on a floured surface. Cut off and reserve ½- to ¾-inch strips from each side. Place pastry square on a baking sheet sprayed with cooking spray. Dampen edges of pastry square lightly with water. Lay reserved strips of pastry over edges of pastry square, forming a shell with raised edges. Press strips lightly to seal.

SPREAD pesto evenly across bottom of pastry shell; sprinkle with ½ cup cheese, tomato slices and remaining ½ cup cheese.

BAKE in preheated 400°F oven for 17 to 20 minutes or until golden brown. Serve immediately. *Makes 9 servings*

Hints from Hunt's®: No need to fear working with puff pastry. It is easy to thaw and use. Do not confuse puff pastry with phyllo pastry, which is more delicate.

Hunt's® Easy Bruschetta

Prep Time: 5 minutes • **Cook Time:** 10 minutes

1 French baguette (18 inches long), cut into ¾-inch slices
¼ cup virgin olive oil, divided
1 can (14.5 ounces) HUNT'S® Petite Diced Tomatoes, drained
1 tablespoon minced garlic
1 package (⅔ ounces) fresh basil, chopped (about ⅓ cup)

PLACE slices of bread on a baking sheet; brush tops with 2 tablespoons olive oil. Bake in a preheated 350°F oven for about 10 minutes or until lightly toasted.

COMBINE tomatoes, garlic, remaining 2 tablespoons olive oil and basil in a small bowl. Season to taste with salt and pepper.

SPREAD tomato mixture evenly over toasted bread. Serve immediately.

Makes 12 servings

Artichoke Crostini

1 jar (6 ounces) marinated artichoke hearts, drained and chopped
3 green onions, chopped
5 tablespoons grated Parmesan cheese, divided
2 tablespoons mayonnaise
12 slices French bread (½ inch thick)

1. Preheat broiler. Combine artichokes, green onions, 3 tablespoons cheese and mayonnaise in small bowl; mix well. Set aside.

2. Arrange bread slices on baking sheet. Broil 4 to 5 inches from heat 2 to 3 minutes on each side or until lightly browned.

3. Spread about 1 tablespoon artichoke mixture onto each bread slice; sprinkle with remaining 2 tablespoons cheese. Broil 1 to 2 minutes or until cheese is melted and lightly browned. *Makes 4 servings*

Sicilian Caponata

5 tablespoons olive or vegetable oil, divided
8 cups (1½ pounds) cubed unpeeled eggplant
2½ cups onion slices
1 cup chopped celery
1 can (14.5 ounces) CONTADINA® Recipe Ready Diced Tomatoes with Roasted Garlic, undrained
⅓ cup chopped pitted ripe olives, drained
¼ cup balsamic or red wine vinegar
2 tablespoons capers
2 teaspoons granulated sugar
½ teaspoon salt
Dash of ground black pepper

1. Heat 3 tablespoons oil in large skillet. Add eggplant; sauté 6 minutes. Remove eggplant from skillet.

2. Heat remaining oil in same skillet. Add onions and celery; sauté 5 minutes or until vegetables are tender.

3. Stir in undrained tomatoes and eggplant; cover. Simmer 15 minutes or until eggplant is tender.

4. Stir in olives, vinegar, capers, sugar, salt and pepper; simmer, uncovered, 5 minutes, stirring occasionally. Serve with toasted bread slices, if desired   *Makes 4½ cups*

Grilled Shrimp Bruschetta

Prep Time: 15 minutes • **Cook Time:** 5 minutes

- **8 vine-ripened tomatoes, seeded and chopped**
- **2 cups CRISCO® Canola Oil*, divided**
- **½ cup chopped fresh rosemary leaves, divided, plus additional for garnish**
- **2 tablespoons red wine vinegar, divided**
- **Salt and pepper**
- **16 large shrimp, peeled and deveined**
- **8 thick slices crusty Italian bread**
- **CRISCO® No-Stick Cooking Spray**
- **2 garlic cloves, peeled, cut in half**

*Or use your favorite Crisco Oil.

Place tomatoes in bowl with 1 cup CRISCO Oil, ¼ cup rosemary leaves and 1 tablespoon vinegar. Season to taste with salt and pepper and marinate for 30 minutes. In separate bowl, marinate shrimp in remaining 1 cup CRISCO Oil, ¼ cup rosemary leaves and 1 tablespoon vinegar. Season to taste with salt and pepper and marinate for 30 minutes.

Drain shrimp (discard marinade) and grill or broil on both sides.

Preheat oven to 350°F. Place bread slices on baking sheet. Spray both sides of bread with CRISCO Cooking Spray. Rub one side of each piece with cut garlic. Season to taste with salt and pepper. Bake 5 minutes or until light golden brown.

Top toast with tomatoes and shrimp; garnish with rosemary.

Makes 4 servings

Awesome Antipasto

1 jar (16 ounces) mild cherry peppers, drained
1 jar (9 ounces) artichoke hearts, drained
½ pound asparagus spears, cooked
½ cup pitted black olives
1 red onion, cut into thin wedges
1 green bell pepper, sliced into rings
1 red bell pepper, sliced into rings
1 bottle (8 ounces) Italian salad dressing
1 cup shredded Parmesan cheese, divided
1 package (6 ounces) HILLSHIRE FARM® Hard Salami

Layer cherry peppers, artichoke hearts, asparagus, olives, onion and bell peppers in 13×9-inch glass baking dish.

Pour dressing and ⅓ cup cheese over vegetables. Cover; refrigerate 1 to 2 hours.

Drain vegetables, reserving marinade. Arrange vegetables and Hard Salami in rows on serving platter. Drizzle with reserved marinade. Top with remaining ⅔ cup cheese.   *Makes 6 servings*

*Quick Tip

If you have leftover antipasto, you're in luck! It makes a great sandwich filling inside a roll or between slices of crusty Italian bread. Or, chop the leftovers and toss them with cooked pasta for a deliciously simple pasta salad.

Easy Tomato Minestrone　　　　　　　　**Rigatoni Salad**

Tomato-Fresh Mozzarella Salad

Panzanella

Soups & Salads

Italian Tortellini Salad

2 cups broccoli florets
½ cup sliced carrots
8 ounces tortellini, cooked and cooled
1 cup (6 ounces) CURE 81® ham, cut into strips
1 cup sliced green bell pepper
1 cup sliced red bell pepper
½ cup sliced red onion
½ cup creamy Italian salad dressing

Cook broccoli and carrots in boiling water 2 to 3 minutes or until crisp-tender; drain. Cool. In large bowl, combine broccoli, carrots, cooked tortellini, ham, bell peppers and onion. Toss with dressing.

Makes 4 servings

Ravioli Soup

Prep and Cook Time: 15 minutes

1 package (9 ounces) fresh or frozen cheese ravioli or tortellini
¾ pound hot Italian sausage, crumbled
1 can (14½ ounces) DEL MONTE® Stewed Tomatoes - Seasoned with Basil, Garlic & Oregano
1 can (14½ ounces) beef broth
1 can (14½ ounces) DEL MONTE® Italian Beans, drained
2 green onions, sliced

1. Cook pasta according to package directions; drain.

2. Meanwhile, cook sausage in 5-quart pot over medium-high heat until no longer pink; drain. Add undrained tomatoes, broth and 1¾ cups water; bring to a boil.

3. Reduce heat to low; stir in pasta, beans and green onions. Simmer until heated through. Season with pepper and sprinkle with grated Parmesan cheese, if desired.

Makes 4 servings

Easy Tomato Minestrone

3 slices bacon, diced
½ cup chopped onion
1 large garlic clove, pressed
3½ cups water
2 cans (10½ ounces each) beef broth, undiluted
1 can (15 ounces) Great Northern beans, undrained
1 can (6 ounces) CONTADINA® Tomato Paste
¼ cup chopped fresh parsley
1 teaspoon dried oregano leaves, crushed
1 teaspoon dried basil leaves, crushed
¼ teaspoon pepper
½ cup dry pasta shells, macaroni or vermicelli, broken into
    1-inch pieces
1 package (16 ounces) frozen mixed Italian vegetables
½ cup grated Parmesan cheese (optional)

1. Sauté bacon, onion and garlic in large saucepan until onion is translucent.

2. Stir in water, broth, beans and liquid, tomato paste, parsley, oregano, basil, pepper and pasta; heat to boiling.

3. Reduce heat; simmer 15 minutes. Mix in vegetables; cook additional 10 minutes. Serve with Parmesan cheese, if desired.

Makes about 8 servings

Four-Season Pasta Salad

8 ounces uncooked trumpet-shaped or spiral pasta
1½ cups cauliflower florets
1½ cups sliced carrots
1½ cups snow peas
½ cup prepared Italian or honey-mustard salad dressing

1. Cook pasta according to package directions, adding cauliflower, carrots and snow peas to saucepan 3 minutes before end of cooking time. Drain pasta and vegetables; run under cold water to stop cooking and drain again. Transfer to large bowl.

2. Add salad dressing; toss lightly to coat.   *Makes 4 to 6 servings*

Italian Peasant Salad

Prep Time: 10 minutes • **Cook Time:** 25 minutes

1 (6.9-ounce) package RICE-A-RONI® Chicken Flavor
2 tablespoons vegetable oil
1 (16-ounce) can cannellini beans, Great Northern beans or navy beans, rinsed and drained
2 cups chopped cooked chicken
2 medium tomatoes, chopped
1 cup frozen or canned peas, drained
½ cup Italian dressing
1 teaspoon dried basil *or* ½ teaspoon dried rosemary leaves, crushed

1. In large skillet over medium heat, sauté rice-vermicelli mix with oil until vermicelli is golden brown.

2. Slowly stir in 2½ cups water and Special Seasonings; bring to a boil. Reduce heat to low. Cover; simmer 15 to 20 minutes or until rice is tender. Cool 10 minutes.

3. In large bowl, combine rice mixture, beans, chicken, tomatoes, peas, Italian dressing and basil. Cover; chill 1 hour.   *Makes 6 servings*

Hearty Tortellini Soup

Prep Time: 15 minutes • **Cook Time:** 10 minutes

2 tablespoons oil
1 small red onion, chopped
2 medium carrots, chopped
2 ribs celery, thinly sliced
1 small zucchini, chopped
2 plum tomatoes, chopped
2 cloves garlic, minced
2 cans (14½ ounces each) chicken broth
1 can (15 to 19 ounces) red kidney beans, rinsed and drained
½ cup water
2 tablespoons *French's*® Worcestershire Sauce
1 package (9 ounces) refrigerated tortellini pasta

1. Heat oil in 6-quart saucepot or Dutch oven over medium-high heat. Add vegetables, tomatoes and garlic. Cook and stir 5 minutes or until vegetables are crisp-tender.

2. Add broth, beans, water and Worcestershire. Heat to boiling. Stir in pasta. Return to boiling. Cook 5 minutes or until pasta is tender, stirring occasionally. Serve with crusty bread and grated Parmesan cheese, if desired.   *Makes 4 servings*

Panzanella

Prep Time: 20 minutes • **Chill Time:** 2 hours

**1 package KNORR® Recipe Classics™ Tomato with Basil
    Soup, Dip and Recipe Mix**
½ cup BERTOLLI® Classico™ Olive Oil
½ cup red wine vinegar
**1 package (16 ounces) frozen tortellini, cooked and
    drained (reserve ¼ cup pasta water)**
3 cups day-old or toasted bread cubes
1 cup sliced pepperoni (4 ounces)
**4 ounces provolone cheese, cut into ½-inch cubes
    (about 1 cup)**
⅓ cup pitted Kalamata olives, sliced
¼ cup thinly sliced red onion

In large bowl, combine recipe mix, olive oil, vinegar and reserved pasta water. Add remaining ingredients; toss to coat. Chill 2 hours.

Makes 6 servings

Balsamic Pasta Salad

Prep Time: 15 minutes • **Cook Time:** 10 minutes

**8 ounces uncooked rotini pasta, cooked according to
    package directions and kept warm**
1 bag (16 ounces) frozen mixed vegetables, thawed, drained
1 can (15 ounces) kidney beans, drained, rinsed
½ large green bell pepper, diced
**2 cans (14.5 ounces each) HUNT'S® Diced Tomatoes with
    Balsamic Vinegar, Basil & Olive Oil, undrained**
¼ cup shredded Parmesan cheese

COMBINE pasta, vegetables, kidney beans and bell pepper in a large bowl.

ADD tomatoes; toss to coat. Sprinkle with Parmesan cheese; blend well. Serve warm or cold. *Makes 5 to 6 servings*

Sicilian-Style Pasta Salad

1 pound dry rotini pasta
2 cans (14.5 ounces each) CONTADINA® Recipe Ready
Diced Tomatoes with Italian Herbs, undrained
1 cup sliced yellow bell pepper
1 cup sliced zucchini
8 ounces cooked bay shrimp
1 can (2.25 ounces) sliced pitted ripe olives, drained
2 tablespoons balsamic vinegar

1. Cook pasta according to package directions; drain.

2. Combine pasta, undrained tomatoes, bell pepper, zucchini, shrimp, olives and vinegar in large bowl; toss well.

3. Cover. Chill before serving. *Makes 10 servings*

Simple Summer Pasta Salad

8 ounces uncooked bow tie pasta
2 large ripe tomatoes, seeded and chopped
1 package (8 ounces) fresh mozzarella cheese, cut into
½-inch pieces
1 can (6 ounces) tuna packed in water, drained
⅓ cup coarsely chopped fresh basil leaves
1 clove garlic, minced
¾ cup Italian salad dressing
Black pepper

1. Cook pasta according to package directions; drain.

2. Combine tomatoes, mozzarella, tuna, basil and garlic in large bowl; toss gently. Add pasta and salad dressing; toss lightly to coat. Season with pepper to taste. Refrigerate before serving. *Makes 6 to 8 servings*

Chick-Pea and Shrimp Soup

1 tablespoon olive or vegetable oil
1 cup diced onion
2 cloves garlic, minced
4 cans (10.5 ounces each) beef broth
1 can (14.5 ounces) CONTADINA® Recipe Ready Diced Tomatoes with Roasted Garlic, undrained
1 can (15 ounces) chick-peas (garbanzo beans), drained
1 can (6 ounces) CONTADINA Italian Paste with Italian Seasonings
8 ounces small cooked shrimp
2 tablespoons chopped fresh Italian parsley *or* 2 teaspoons dried parsley flakes, crushed
½ teaspoon salt
¼ teaspoon ground black pepper

1. Heat oil over medium-high heat in large saucepan. Add onion and garlic; sauté for 1 minute.

2. Stir in broth, undrained tomatoes, chick-peas and tomato paste. Bring to a boil.

3. Reduce heat to low; simmer, uncovered, 10 minutes. Add shrimp, parsley, salt and pepper; simmer 3 minutes or until heated through. Stir before serving.   *Makes 8 to 10 servings*

*Quick Tip

Italian parsley (also called flat leaf parsley) has a stronger flavor than curly parsley. Both kinds of parsley should be washed well and stemmed before using. Drying the leaves thoroughly will make chopping them much easier.

Tomato-Fresh Mozzarella Salad

Vinaigrette Dressing (recipe follows)
1 pound fresh mozzarella
1 pound ripe tomatoes
Fresh whole large basil leaves as needed
Salt and black pepper

Prepare Vinaigrette Dressing. Cut mozzarella into ¼-inch slices. Cut tomatoes into ¼-inch slices. Alternate mozzarella slices, tomato slices and basil leaves overlapping on plate. Drizzle with dressing. Sprinkle with salt and pepper. *Makes 4 servings*

Vinaigrette Dressing

1 tablespoon balsamic or wine vinegar
¼ teaspoon Dijon mustard
Pinch of salt, black pepper and sugar
¼ cup olive oil

Whisk together vinegar, mustard, salt, pepper and sugar in small bowl until smooth. Add oil in thin stream, whisking until mixture is smooth. Refrigerate until ready to use. Whisk again before serving.

Quick Tuscan Bean, Tomato and Spinach Soup

2 cans (14½ ounces each) diced tomatoes with onions
1 can (14½ ounces) reduced-sodium chicken broth
2 teaspoons sugar
2 teaspoons dried basil
¾ teaspoon Worcestershire sauce
1 can (15 ounces) small white beans, rinsed and drained
3 ounces fresh baby spinach leaves or chopped spinach leaves, stems removed
1 tablespoon extra-virgin olive oil

1. Combine tomatoes, broth, sugar, basil and Worcestershire sauce in Dutch oven or large saucepan; bring to a boil over high heat. Reduce heat and simmer, uncovered, 10 minutes.

2. Stir in beans and spinach; cook 5 minutes longer or until spinach is tender.

3. Remove from heat; stir in oil just before serving.

Makes 4 (1½-cup) servings

BelGioioso® Parmesan-Mushroom Salad

3 ounces BELGIOIOSO® Parmesan
½ pound firm, fresh mushrooms
1 cup thinly sliced celery
6 tablespoons olive oil
2 tablespoons fresh lemon juice
1 teaspoon salt
⅛ teaspoon freshly ground black pepper

Slice BelGioioso Parmesan very thinly. Trim mushrooms; cut vertically into thin slices. Toss cheese, mushrooms and celery with mixture of oil and lemon juice. Season with salt and pepper. *Makes 4 to 6 servings*

Rigatoni
Salad

12 ounces uncooked rigatoni pasta, cooked
1 package (10 ounces) frozen snow peas or sugar snap peas, thawed
1 to 2 cups chopped greens, such as arugula, frisée or any crisp lettuce
8 ounces cherry tomatoes, cut into halves
1 medium red or yellow bell pepper, cut into thin strips
½ red onion, cut into thin strips
⅓ cup sliced black olives
⅓ to ½ cup Italian salad dressing
Grated Parmesan cheese (optional)

Combine all ingredients except cheese in large salad bowl. Toss gently to mix and coat all ingredients. Sprinkle with cheese, if desired.

Makes about 8 servings

Note: Vary the amounts of each ingredient according to your taste. Substitute steamed green beans (whole or cut) for the peas or add steamed, sliced carrots, zucchini or yellow squash.

Hearty Bean & Pasta Soup

1 cup uncooked elbow macaroni
2 tablespoons olive oil
1 medium onion, chopped
2 cloves garlic, minced
4 cups water
2 cans (14½ ounces each) reduced-sodium chicken broth
1 jar (26 ounces) marinara sauce
1 can (15 ounces) Great Northern or cannellini beans,
  rinsed and drained
2 teaspoons balsamic vinegar
1 pound fresh spinach, chopped
½ cup grated Parmesan cheese (optional)

1. Cook pasta according to package directions; drain.

2. Meanwhile, heat oil in Dutch oven or large saucepan over medium heat. Add onion and garlic; cook and stir 5 minutes or until onion is tender.

3. Stir in water, broth, marinara sauce and beans; bring to a boil. Reduce heat to low; cook, uncovered, 10 minutes, stirring occasionally. Stir in spinach and cooked pasta; cook 5 minutes. Sprinkle with cheese before serving.   *Makes 10 to 12 servings*

*Quick Tip

To save time, use fresh baby spinach leaves instead of regular spinach. Prewashed baby spinach is available in packages in the supermarket produce section; the leaves can be added to the soup whole so that chopping isn't necessary.

Hearty Italian Minestrone

Prep Time: 20 minutes • **Total Time:** 1¼ hours

7 cups water
2½ tablespoons HERB-OX® reduced sodium beef flavored bouillon
2 cups coarsely chopped cabbage
1 (14½-ounce) can diced tomatoes with basil, garlic and oregano
1 medium onion, chopped
1 medium carrot, halved lengthwise and diagonally sliced
1 tablespoon Italian seasoning
1½ cups frozen French cut green beans
1 zucchini, halved lengthwise and cut into chunks
½ cup ditilini or small shell pasta
1 (15-ounce) can red kidney beans, drained
1 cup HORMEL® sliced pepperoni, quartered
Garlic salt and pepper, to taste
Refrigerated prepared pesto (optional)
Shredded Parmesan cheese (optional)

In large stockpot, combine first seven ingredients. Bring to a boil. Reduce heat to low and simmer, partially covered, for 20 minutes. Add green beans, zucchini and pasta. Simmer, uncovered, for an additional 15 minutes or until vegetables and pasta are tender. Stir in beans and pepperoni. Heat until warmed through, about 2 minutes. Season to taste with garlic salt and pepper. If desired, serve with pesto and Parmesan cheese.

Makes 10 servings

Basic Olive Oil Vinaigrette

⅓ cup wine or cider vinegar
¼ teaspoon salt
¼ teaspoon black pepper
1 cup FILIPPO BERIO® Extra Virgin Olive Oil

Whisk together vinegar, salt and pepper in small bowl. Slowly whisk in oil until well blended. Serve with salad greens. *Makes 10 servings*

Herb Vinaigrette: Prepare as directed. Stir in 1 teaspoon each dried mustard, basil and tarragon leaves.

Balsamic Vinaigrette: Prepare as directed, substituting balsamic vinegar for wine vinegar. Stir in 1 tablespoon minced shallots and ¼ teaspoon dried marjoram leaves.

Chive Vinaigrette: Prepare as directed. Stir in 2 teaspoons minced fresh chives.

Creamy Dijon Vinaigrette: Prepare as directed. Whisk in 2 teaspoons Dijon mustard and ½ tablespoon mayonnaise.

Honey-Dijon Vinaigrette: Prepare as directed. Whisk in 1 tablespoon Dijon mustard and 2 tablespoons honey.

Mint Vinaigrette: Prepare as directed. Stir in 2 tablespoons chopped fresh mint.

Parmesan Vinaigrette: Prepare as directed. Stir in 1 tablespoon Parmesan cheese.

Raspberry Vinaigrette: Prepare as directed, substituting raspberry vinegar for wine vinegar.

Sesame Vinaigrette: Prepare as directed, substituting rice vinegar for wine vinegar. Stir in 2 cloves minced garlic and 2 tablespoons toasted sesame seeds.

Chicken Pesto Pizza

BelGioioso® Asiago and
Sweet Pepper Sandwich

Grilled Panini Sandwich

Rustic Tuscany Bread

Sandwiches & Pizza

Savory Onion Focaccia

Prep Time: 30 minutes • **Cook Time:** 27 minutes

1 **pound frozen pizza or bread dough***
1 **tablespoon olive oil**
1 **clove garlic, minced**
1⅓ **cups** *French's®* **French Fried Onions, divided**
1 **cup (4 ounces) shredded mozzarella cheese**
½ **pound plum tomatoes (4 small), thinly sliced**
2 **teaspoons fresh chopped rosemary** *or* ½ **teaspoon dried rosemary**
3 **tablespoons grated Parmesan cheese**

*Pizza dough can be found in the frozen section of the supermarket. Thaw in the refrigerator before using.

1. Bring pizza dough to room temperature. Grease 15×10-inch jelly-roll pan. Roll or pat dough into rectangle same size as pan on floured board.** Transfer dough to pan.

2. Combine oil and garlic in small bowl; brush onto surface of dough. Cover loosely with kitchen towel. Let dough rise at room temperature 25 minutes. Prick dough with fork.

3. Preheat oven to 450°F. Bake dough 20 minutes or until edges and bottom of crust are golden. Sprinkle *1 cup* French Fried Onions and mozzarella cheese over dough. Arrange tomatoes over cheese; sprinkle with rosemary. Bake 5 minutes or until cheese melts.

4. Sprinkle with remaining ⅓ *cup* onions and Parmesan cheese. Bake 2 minutes or until onions are golden. To serve, cut into rectangles.

Makes 8 appetizer servings

**If dough is too hard to roll, allow to rest on floured board.

BelGioioso® Asiago and Sweet Pepper Sandwiches

2 tablespoons olive oil
1 red bell pepper, sliced into strips
1 yellow bell pepper, sliced into strips
1 medium onion, thinly sliced
1 teaspoon dried thyme
  Hot pepper sauce
  Salt and pepper to taste
4 ounces BELGIOIOSO® Asiago Cheese, thinly sliced
4 crusty Italian sandwich rolls, split lengthwise

Heat olive oil in large skillet. Add red and yellow bell peppers and cook over medium heat about 6 minutes. Add onion and cook until vegetables are softened. Stir in thyme, hot pepper sauce, salt and pepper to taste.

Layer BelGioioso Asiago Cheese on bottom half of rolls and top with vegetable mixture. Serve immediately. *Makes 4 servings*

Pizza Romano

1 (10-inch) prepared pizza crust *or* 4 rounds pita bread
1 cup (4 ounces) shredded mozzarella cheese
4 slices HILLSHIRE FARM® Ham, cut into ½-inch strips
1 jar (8 ounces) marinated sun-dried tomatoes, drained (optional)
1 jar (6 ounces) oil-packed artichokes, drained and cut into eighths
1 jar (4 ounces) roasted red peppers, drained and cut into strips

Preheat oven to 425°F.

Place pizza crust on cookie sheet; top with remaining ingredients. Bake on lower rack of oven 15 to 20 minutes or until crust begins to brown lightly and cheese is melted. *Makes 4 servings*

Chicken Pesto
Pizza

Cornmeal
1 loaf (1 pound) frozen bread dough, thawed
Nonstick cooking spray
8 ounces chicken tenders, cut into ½-inch pieces
½ red onion, cut into quarters and thinly sliced
¼ cup prepared pesto
2 large plum tomatoes, seeded and diced
1 cup (4 ounces) shredded pizza cheese blend or mozzarella cheese

1. Preheat oven to 375°F. Sprinkle baking sheet with cornmeal. Roll out bread dough on floured surface to 14×8-inch rectangle. Transfer to prepared baking sheet. Cover loosely with plastic wrap; let rise 20 to 30 minutes.

2. Meanwhile, spray large skillet with cooking spray; heat over medium heat. Add chicken; cook and stir 2 minutes. Add onion and pesto; cook and stir 3 to 4 minutes or until chicken is cooked through. Stir in tomatoes. Remove from heat; let cool slightly.

3. Spread chicken mixture evenly over dough to within 1 inch of edges. Sprinkle with cheese.

4. Bake on bottom rack of oven about 20 minutes or until crust is golden brown. Cut into 2-inch squares.   *Makes about 20 squares*

Grilled Panini Sandwiches

8 slices country Italian, sourdough or other firm-textured bread
8 slices SARGENTO® Deli Style Sliced Mozzarella Cheese
⅓ cup prepared pesto
4 large slices ripe tomato
2 tablespoons olive oil

1. Top each of 4 slices of bread with 1 slice of cheese. Spread pesto over cheese. Arrange tomatoes on top, then another slice of cheese. Close sandwiches with remaining 4 slices of bread.

2. Brush olive oil lightly over both sides of sandwiches. Cook sandwiches over medium-low coals or in preheated ridged grill pan over medium heat 3 to 4 minutes per side or until bread is toasted and cheese is melted.

Makes 4 servings

Warm Focaccia Pizza Bread

½ cup HELLMANN'S® or BEST FOODS® Real Mayonnaise
¼ cup plus 2 tablespoons shredded mozzarella cheese
2 tablespoons grated Parmesan cheese
1 tablespoon thinly sliced fresh basil leaves
6 ounces cooked chicken, sliced (about 1⅓ cups)
6 slices tomato
2 (6-inch) prebaked pizza crusts

Preheat oven to 450°F.

In medium bowl, combine Hellmann's or Best Foods Real Mayonnaise, ¼ cup mozzarella cheese, Parmesan cheese and basil. Stir in chicken.

Evenly spread on pizza crusts, then top with tomato and remaining 2 tablespoons mozzarella cheese. Arrange on baking sheet.

Bake 15 minutes or until crust is golden brown and cheese is melted.

Makes 4 servings

Grilled Panini Sandwich

Plum Tomato Basil Pizza

1 cup (4 ounces) shredded mozzarella cheese
1 (10-ounce) package prepared pizza crust
4 ripe seeded Italian plum tomatoes, sliced
½ cup fresh basil leaves
1½ teaspoons TABASCO® brand Pepper Sauce
   Olive oil

Preheat oven to 425°F. Sprinkle shredded mozzarella cheese evenly over pizza crust. Layer with tomatoes and basil. Drizzle with TABASCO® Sauce and olive oil. Bake on pizza pan or stone 15 minutes or until cheese is melted and crust is golden brown. *Makes 4 servings*

Pepperoni-Oregano Focaccia

1 tablespoon cornmeal
1 can (10 ounces) refrigerated pizza crust dough
½ cup finely chopped pepperoni (3 to 3½ ounces)
1½ teaspoons finely chopped fresh oregano *or* ½ teaspoon
   dried oregano leaves
2 teaspoons olive oil

1. Preheat oven to 425°F. Grease large baking sheet; sprinkle with cornmeal.

2. Unroll dough onto lightly floured surface. Pat dough into 12×9-inch rectangle. Sprinkle half of pepperoni and half of oregano over one side of dough. Fold over dough, making 12×4½-inch rectangle.

3. Roll dough into 12×9-inch rectangle. Place on prepared baking sheet. Prick dough with fork at 2-inch intervals about 30 times. Brush with oil; sprinkle with remaining pepperoni and oregano.

4. Bake 12 to 15 minutes or until golden brown. (Prick dough several more times if dough puffs as it bakes.) Cut into strips.

Makes 12 servings

Mozzarella-Prosciutto Panini

1 BAYS® English Muffin, split
½ teaspoon bottled Italian dressing
¼ ounce prosciutto
Thinly sliced Roma tomato
1½ ounces smoked mozzarella, sliced to fit inside of muffin
1 teaspoon softened butter

Preheat heavy skillet or griddle over low heat until spatter of water disappears quickly. Sprinkle each half of muffin with Italian dressing. Stack prosciutto, tomato and smoked mozzarella on bottom of muffin. Replace top. Spread softened butter on outside of sandwich.

Place sandwich bottom side down in preheated skillet. Place heavy saucepan weighted with 2 canned goods or brick wrapped in heavy duty foil on top to flatten. Cook 3 minutes. Turn and cook on second side 3 minutes with weight in place until cheese starts to sizzle into pan. Remove weight and finish cooking. *Makes 1 serving*

Turkey Cheddar Panini: For each panini, spread bottom half of muffin with 2 teaspoons chutney; top with ½ ounce sliced turkey or cooked roast pork, 1 ounce Cheddar cheese and top half of muffin. Spread 1 teaspoon softened butter on outside of sandwich. Cook 3 minutes per side as directed above.

Fontina-Caponata Panini: For each panini, spread bottom half of muffin with rounded tablespoonful of prepared caponata (eggplant appetizer); top with 1½ ounces Fontina or smoked mozzarella sliced to fit muffin and top half of muffin. Spread 1 teaspoon softened butter on outside of sandwich. Cook 3 minutes per side as directed above.

Tomato-Feta Focaccia

1 package (16 ounces) frozen bread dough, thawed
2 plum tomatoes, thinly sliced
1 cup (4 ounces) crumbled feta cheese
1 tablespoon chopped fresh rosemary *or* 1 teaspoon dried rosemary

1. Coat 15×10-inch jelly-roll pan and hands with nonstick cooking spray. Place dough in pan; press gently to edges. (If dough won't stretch to edges of pan, let rest 5 minutes.) Cover with plastic wrap; let stand in warm place about 30 minutes or until doubled in bulk.

2. Preheat oven to 375°F. Arrange tomatoes in single layer over dough. Sprinkle with cheese and rosemary. Bake 23 to 25 minutes or until bottom is crisp and top is well browned. To further brown top, place in broiler 1 to 2 minutes. *Makes 15 servings*

Pizza Blanco

½ cup grated Parmesan cheese
1 (12-inch) prebaked pizza crust
3 plum tomatoes, thinly sliced
½ cup HIDDEN VALLEY® The Original Ranch® Dressing
½ cup roasted red pepper strips, rinsed and drained
1 can (2¼ ounces) sliced ripe olives, drained
¼ cup sliced green onions
1 cup (4 ounces) shredded mozzarella and Cheddar cheese blend

Preheat oven to 450°F. Sprinkle Parmesan cheese on pizza crust; cover with single layer of tomato slices. Drizzle dressing over tomatoes. Arrange red pepper, olives and onions on pizza; sprinkle with cheese blend. Bake at 450°F for 15 minutes or until cheese is melted and crust is hot.

Makes 8 servings

Panini with Fresh Mozzarella and Basil

½ **cup prepared vinaigrette**
1 **loaf (16 ounces) Italian bread, cut in half lengthwise**
6 **ounces fresh mozzarella cheese, cut into 12 slices**
8 **ounces thinly sliced oven roasted deli turkey**
12 **to 16 fresh whole basil leaves**
1 **large tomato, thinly sliced**
½ **cup thinly sliced red onion (optional)**
⅛ **teaspoon red pepper flakes**

1. Preheat indoor grill.

2. Brush vinaigrette evenly over both cut sides of bread. Arrange cheese evenly over bottom half of bread; top with turkey, basil, tomato and onion. Sprinkle evenly with red pepper flakes. Cover with top half of bread and press down firmly. Cut crosswise into 4 sandwiches.

3. Place sandwiches on grill (family-size grill will cook two sandwiches at a time); close lid and cook 5 to 7 minutes or until cheese melts.

4. Place on serving platter and cover lightly with foil. Repeat with remaining sandwiches. *Makes 4 servings*

Rustic Tuscany Bread

Prep Time: 30 minutes • Cook Time: 20 to 30 minutes

1 pound frozen bread dough
1 tablespoon olive oil
¼ teaspoon salt
¼ teaspoon cracked black pepper
1 can (14.5 ounces) HUNT'S® Diced Tomatoes with Basil,
** Garlic & Oregano, drained**
½ cup (2 ounces) shredded Cheddar cheese
½ cup (2 ounces) shredded mozzarella cheese
** PAM® No Stick Cooking Spray**

THAW bread dough; let rise according to package directions.

ROLL dough out to a 12×10-inch rectangle. Brush dough lightly with olive oil; sprinkle with salt and pepper. Layer well-drained tomatoes and cheeses over dough. Fold dough in thirds over filling. With a sharp knife, make three diagonal cuts, about 2 inches apart, on top of dough through first layer. Repeat with second set of cuts in opposite direction, crisscrossing first cuts.

PLACE dough on a baking sheet coated with cooking spray. Bake in a preheated 400°F oven for 25 minutes or until golden brown.

Makes 6 servings

*Quick Tip

Purchase pepper and other spices in small amounts to insure their freshness. Black pepper should be kept in a tightly sealed glass container in a cool, dark and dry place. Whole peppercorns will keep almost indefinitely, while ground pepper will stay fresh for about three months.

Chicken and Linguine in Creamy Tomato Sauce

Skillet Pasta Roma

Traditional Spaghetti Sauce

Rigatoni with Sausage & Beans

Everyday **Pasta**

Zesty Artichoke Pesto Sauce

Prep Time: 5 minutes • **Cook Time:** 19 minutes

1 jar (6 ounces) marinated artichoke hearts, chopped, marinade reserved
1 cup sliced onion
1 can (14.5 ounces) CONTADINA® Recipe Ready Diced Tomatoes, undrained
1 can (6 ounces) CONTADINA Italian Paste with Pesto
1 cup water
½ teaspoon salt
Hot cooked pasta

1. Heat reserved artichoke marinade in large saucepan over medium-high heat until warm.

2. Add onion; cook for 3 to 4 minutes or until tender. Add artichoke hearts, tomatoes and juice, tomato paste, water and salt.

3. Bring to a boil; reduce heat to low. Cook, stirring occasionally, for 10 to 15 minutes or until flavors are blended. Serve over pasta.

Makes 6 to 8 servings

Savory Caper and Olive Sauce: Eliminate artichoke hearts. Heat 2 tablespoons olive oil in large saucepan over medium-high heat. Add onion; cook for 3 to 4 minutes or until tender. Add tomatoes and juice, tomato paste, water, salt, ¾ cup sliced and quartered zucchini, ½ cup (2¼-ounce can) drained sliced ripe olives and 2 tablespoons capers. Proceed as above.

Chunky Tomato Alfredo Linguine

Prep Time: 15 minutes • Cook Time: 5 minutes

1 can (14.5 ounces) HUNT'S® Diced Tomatoes in Juice, undrained
1 can (6 ounces) HUNT'S® Tomato Paste
1 container (10 ounces) refrigerated Alfredo sauce
1 pound uncooked linguine pasta, cooked and kept warm

COMBINE tomatoes and paste in a microwave-safe bowl; heat on HIGH 2 to 3 minutes, stirring halfway through.

FOLD in Alfredo sauce; toss with linguine.

Makes 6 servings (about 1⅓ cups each)

Tuscan-Style Fettuccine with Artichokes

½ cup (1 stick) I CAN'T BELIEVE IT'S NOT BUTTER!® Spread
1 can (14 ounces) artichoke hearts, drained and chopped
⅓ cup chopped fresh cilantro (optional)
2 tablespoons chopped fresh oregano leaves *or* 1 teaspoon dried oregano leaves, crushed
2 tablespoons finely chopped garlic
½ teaspoon ground black pepper
1 box (16 ounces) fettuccine, cooked and drained
 Grated Parmesan cheese

In 12-inch skillet, melt I Can't Believe It's Not Butter!® Spread over medium-high heat and cook artichokes, cilantro, oregano, garlic and pepper, stirring occasionally, 3 minutes or until heated through. To serve, toss sauce with hot fettuccine and sprinkle with cheese.

Makes 6 servings

Fusilli with Fresh Red & Yellow Tomato Sauce

½ cup (1 stick) I CAN'T BELIEVE IT'S NOT BUTTER!® Spread
1 medium onion, chopped
2 cloves garlic, finely chopped (optional)
1½ pounds red and/or yellow cherry tomatoes, halved
⅓ cup chopped fresh basil leaves
1 box (16 ounces) fusilli (long curly pasta) or linguine, cooked and drained
Grated Parmesan cheese

In 12-inch nonstick skillet, melt I Can't Believe It's Not Butter!® Spread over medium heat and cook onion, stirring occasionally, 2 minutes or until softened. Stir in garlic and tomatoes and cook, stirring occasionally, 5 minutes or until tomatoes soften but do not lose their shape and sauce thickens slightly. Stir in basil and season, if desired, with salt and ground black pepper.

In large serving bowl, toss sauce with hot fusilli and sprinkle with cheese.
Makes 4 servings

Linguine with Red Clam Sauce

1 tablespoon olive oil
2 cloves garlic, finely chopped
1 jar (1 pound 10 ounces) RAGÚ® Old World Style® Pasta Sauce
3 cans (6½ ounces each) minced clams, drained (reserve 1 cup liquid)
Hot pepper sauce to taste (optional)
1 box (16 ounces) linguine, cooked and drained

In 2-quart saucepan, heat olive oil over low heat and cook garlic 30 seconds. Stir in Ragú Pasta Sauce and reserved clam liquid; simmer 5 minutes. Stir in clams and hot pepper sauce; heat through. Spoon sauce over hot linguine. Garnish, if desired, with finely chopped fresh parsley. *Makes 8 servings*

Meaty Mushroom Spaghetti

2 tablespoons olive oil, divided
1 cup chopped onion
2 cloves garlic, minced
1 pound beef top sirloin, cut into ½-inch cubes
8 ounces sliced fresh mushrooms
1 cup chopped green and yellow bell peppers
1 jar (26 ounces) prepared pasta sauce
1 cup canned diced tomatoes, undrained
2 teaspoons dried basil
1 teaspoon dried oregano
1 package (16 ounces) uncooked spaghetti
   Salt and black pepper
   Grated Parmesan cheese

1. Heat 1 tablespoon oil in large skillet over medium heat. Add onion and garlic; cook and stir until onion is tender. Add beef; cook and stir until no longer pink. Add remaining 1 tablespoon oil, mushrooms and bell peppers; cook and stir 2 minutes.

2. Stir in pasta sauce, tomatoes with juice and basil. Cover and simmer 15 to 20 minutes, stirring occasionally.

3. Meanwhile, cook spaghetti according to package directions just until al dente; drain well.

4. Combine hot spaghetti and meat sauce in serving bowl; toss lightly. Season with salt and black pepper; sprinkle with cheese. Serve immediately.   *Makes 6 to 8 servings*

Chicken and Linguine in Creamy Tomato Sauce

Prep Time: 10 minutes • **Cook Time:** 30 minutes

1 tablespoon olive oil
1 pound boneless, skinless chicken breasts, cut into ½-inch strips
1 jar (1 pound 10 ounces) RAGÚ® Old World Style® Pasta Sauce
2 cups water
8 ounces uncooked linguine or spaghetti
½ cup whipping or heavy cream
1 tablespoon chopped fresh basil leaves *or* ½ teaspoon dried basil leaves, crushed

1. In 12-inch skillet, heat olive oil over medium heat and brown chicken. Remove chicken and set aside.

2. In same skillet, stir in Ragú Pasta Sauce and water. Bring to a boil over high heat. Stir in uncooked linguine and return to a boil. Reduce heat to low and simmer covered, stirring occasionally, 15 minutes or until linguine is tender.

3. Stir in cream and basil. Return chicken to skillet and cook 5 minutes or until chicken is thoroughly cooked. *Makes 4 servings*

Baked Pasta
with Ricotta

1 package (16 ounces) uncooked rigatoni or penne pasta
1 container (15 ounces) ricotta cheese
⅔ cup grated Parmesan cheese
2 eggs, lightly beaten
½ teaspoon salt
⅛ teaspoon pepper
2 jars (26 ounces each) marinara sauce, divided
3 cups (12 ounces) shredded mozzarella cheese, divided

1. Preheat oven to 375°F. Spray 13×9-inch baking pan with nonstick cooking spray.

2. Cook rigatoni according to package directions; drain. Meanwhile, beat ricotta, Parmesan, eggs, salt and pepper in medium bowl until well blended.

3. Spread 2 cups marinara sauce over bottom of prepared pan; spoon half of cooked pasta over sauce. Top with half of ricotta mixture and 1 cup mozzarella. Repeat layers of marinara sauce, pasta and ricotta mixture. Top with 1 cup mozzarella, remaining marinara sauce and 1 cup mozzarella.

4. Cover with foil; bake about 1 hour or until bubbly. Uncover and bake about 5 minutes more or until cheese is completely melted. Let stand 15 minutes before serving. *Makes 12 servings*

*Quick Tip
Pasta that is to be baked in a casserole should always be slightly undercooked to prevent it from becoming too soft. Reduce the cooking time by about one third, as the pasta will continue to cook and absorb liquid in the oven.

Pasta
Arrabbiata

Prep Time: 5 minutes • **Cook Time:** 25 minutes

½ cup virgin olive oil
4 teaspoons fresh minced garlic (about 5 cloves)
1 can (28 ounces) HUNT'S® Petite Diced Tomatoes in Juice,
  undrained
1 can (29 ounces) HUNT'S® Tomato Puree
2 teaspoons crushed red pepper
½ teaspoon dried oregano leaves
¼ teaspoon salt
1 pound uncooked penne pasta
½ cup freshly shredded Parmigiano-Reggiano*
¼ cup thinly sliced fresh basil

If not available, substitute a good quality freshly shredded domestic Parmesan cheese.

HEAT oil in a 6-quart saucepan over medium heat. Add garlic; sauté about 3 minutes or until garlic is golden brown. Stir in diced tomatoes and puree; bring to a boil. Reduce heat to low; stir in crushed red pepper, oregano and salt.

COOK, uncovered, for about 20 minutes, stirring occasionally. Meanwhile, prepare pasta according to package directions in a large saucepan. Drain, reserving ½ cup cooking water.

RETURN pasta and reserved water to the saucepan; sprinkle with cheese. Add basil to sauce; pour 2 cups of sauce over pasta. Toss well to combine. Serve pasta with additional sauce. *Makes 6 servings*

Hints from Hunt's®: Tomato Puree has slightly sweet flavor that is ideal for blending flavors and a good addition to the tomato products like diced tomatoes or whole tomatoes to intensify flavors.

Florentine-Stuffed Shells

24 uncooked jumbo pasta shells for filling
1 package (10 ounces) frozen chopped spinach, thawed
2 cups (15 ounces) SARGENTO® Ricotta Cheese*
**1½ cups (6 ounces) SARGENTO® Chef Style or Fancy
   Mozzarella Shredded Cheese**
⅓ cup finely chopped onion
1 egg, slightly beaten
2 cloves garlic, minced
¼ teaspoon salt
⅛ teaspoon ground nutmeg
2 cups meatless spaghetti sauce
**½ cup (2 ounces) SARGENTO® Fancy Parmesan Shredded
   Cheese**

*SARGENTO® Whole Milk Ricotta, Part-Skim Ricotta or Light Ricotta can be used.

Cook pasta shells according to package directions; drain. Meanwhile, squeeze spinach to remove as much moisture as possible. Combine spinach, Ricotta cheese, Mozzarella cheese, onion, egg, garlic, salt and nutmeg; stir to blend well. Stuff shells with Ricotta mixture, using about 2 tablespoons mixture for each shell. Place in lightly greased 13×9-inch baking dish. Pour spaghetti sauce over shells. Sprinkle with Parmesan cheese; cover. Bake at 350°F 30 to 40 minutes or until thoroughly heated.   *Makes 8 servings*

Ravioli with Tomato Pesto

4 ounces frozen cheese ravioli
1¼ cups coarsely chopped plum tomatoes
¼ cup fresh basil leaves
1 tablespoon pine nuts
1 tablespoon olive oil
¼ teaspoon salt
⅛ teaspoon black pepper
2 tablespoons grated Parmesan cheese

1. Cook ravioli according to package directions; drain.

2. Meanwhile, combine tomatoes, basil, pine nuts, oil, salt and pepper in food processor. Process using on/off pulses just until ingredients are chopped. Serve sauce over hot cooked ravioli; top with cheese.

Makes 2 servings

Quick 'n' Easy Pasta Bolognese

½ pound ground beef
2 cloves garlic, finely chopped
1 jar (1 pound 10 ounces) RAGÚ® Chunky Pasta Sauce
¼ cup light cream or half-and-half
3 tablespoons dry white wine (optional)
8 ounces penne or ziti pasta, cooked and drained

In 12-inch skillet, brown ground beef with garlic over medium-high heat; drain. Stir in Ragú Pasta Sauce, cream and wine. Simmer uncovered, stirring occasionally, 15 minutes. Serve over hot pasta and sprinkle, if desired, with grated Parmesan cheese. *Makes 4 servings*

Skillet Pasta Roma

½ pound Italian sausage, sliced or crumbled
1 large onion, coarsely chopped
1 large clove garlic, minced
2 cans (14½ ounces each) DEL MONTE® Diced Tomatoes with Basil, Garlic & Oregano
1 can (8 ounces) DEL MONTE Tomato Sauce
1 cup water
8 ounces uncooked rotini or other spiral pasta
8 mushrooms, sliced (optional)
Grated Parmesan cheese and fresh parsley sprigs (optional)

1. Brown sausage in large skillet. Add onion and garlic. Cook until onion is soft; drain. Stir in undrained tomatoes, tomato sauce, water and pasta.

2. Cover and bring to a boil; reduce heat. Simmer, covered, 25 to 30 minutes or until pasta is tender, stirring occasionally.

3. Stir in mushrooms, if desired; simmer 5 minutes. Serve in skillet garnished with cheese and parsley, if desired.   *Makes 4 servings*

Tuna Linguine

1 (6½-ounce) can white albacore tuna, packed in water
6 tablespoons FILIPPO BERIO® Extra Virgin Olive Oil
Juice of 1 lemon
½ cup chopped fresh parsley
¼ teaspoon black pepper
¼ teaspoon salt (optional)
¾ pound uncooked linguine (or any other pasta)

Drain tuna. In small bowl, break tuna into chunks; add oil. Stir in lemon juice, parsley, pepper and salt, if desired, until combined.

Cook pasta in 4 quarts boiling water for 8 to 9 minutes or according to package directions; do not overcook. Drain. Spoon tuna sauce over pasta in large bowl; toss gently to coat. Serve.   *Makes 4 servings*

Pasta with Fresh Tomato-Olive Sauce

2 tablespoons olive oil
1 small onion, chopped
2 cloves garlic, minced
4 large ripe tomatoes, seeded and chopped (about 3 cups)
¾ teaspoon dried oregano
⅛ teaspoon red pepper flakes
⅔ cup chopped pitted kalamata olives
1 tablespoon capers (optional)
Salt and black pepper
1 package (16 ounces) uncooked spaghetti
Grated Parmesan cheese

1. Heat olive oil in large skillet over medium heat. Add onion and garlic; cook and stir about 4 minutes or until onion is tender.

2. Add tomatoes, oregano and red pepper flakes; simmer, uncovered, 15 to 20 minutes or until sauce is thickened. Stir in olives, capers and salt and pepper to taste.

3. Meanwhile, cook pasta according to package directions; drain. Add pasta to skillet; toss to coat with sauce. Sprinkle with cheese before serving. *Makes 6 to 8 servings*

Tip: If your skillet is not large enough to hold both the sauce and the cooked spaghetti, toss them together in a heated serving bowl.

Rigatoni with Sausage & Beans

Prep Time: 5 minutes • **Cook Time:** 20 minutes

1 pound sweet Italian sausage links, cut into ½-inch pieces
1 jar (1 pound 10 ounces) RAGÚ® Chunky Gardenstyle Pasta Sauce
1 can (19 ounces) cannellini or white kidney beans, rinsed and drained
⅛ to ¼ teaspoon dried rosemary leaves, crushed (optional)
1 box (16 ounces) rigatoni or ziti pasta, cooked and drained

1. In 12-inch skillet, brown sausage over medium-high heat; drain. Stir in Ragú Pasta Sauce, beans and rosemary.

2. Bring to a boil over high heat. Reduce heat to low and simmer uncovered, stirring occasionally, 10 minutes or until sausage is done. Serve over hot pasta. *Makes 4 servings*

Rotini with Cauliflower and Prosciutto

8 ounces uncooked rotini pasta
1 head cauliflower, separated into florets
¼ cup FILIPPO BERIO® Extra Virgin Olive Oil
1 onion, thinly sliced
Salt and freshly ground black pepper
¼ pound thinly sliced prosciutto (preferably imported), cut into bite-size pieces

Cook pasta according to package directions until al dente (tender but still firm). Drain. In large saucepan, cook cauliflower florets in boiling salted water 3 to 5 minutes or until tender. Add to colander with pasta. Drain; transfer to large bowl. In medium saucepan, heat olive oil over medium heat until hot. Add onion; cook and stir 5 to 7 minutes or until tender. Add onion with olive oil to pasta mixture; toss until lightly coated. Season to taste with salt and pepper. Top with prosciutto. *Makes 4 servings*

Quick Pasta Puttanesca

1 package (16 ounces) uncooked spaghetti or linguine
3 tablespoons plus 1 teaspoon olive oil, divided
¼ to 1 teaspoon red pepper flakes*
2 cans (6 ounces each) chunk light tuna packed in water, drained
1 tablespoon dried minced onion
1 teaspoon minced garlic
1 can (28 ounces) diced tomatoes, undrained
1 can (8 ounces) tomato sauce
24 pitted kalamata or ripe olives
2 tablespoons capers, drained

*For a mildly spicy dish, use ¼ teaspoon red pepper. For a very spicy dish, use 1 teaspoon red pepper.

1. Cook spaghetti according to package directions. Drain pasta. Return pasta to saucepan; add 1 teaspoon oil and toss to coat.

2. Meanwhile, heat remaining 3 tablespoons oil in large skillet over medium-high heat. Add red pepper flakes; cook and stir 1 to 2 minutes or until sizzling. Add tuna; cook and stir 2 to 3 minutes. Add onion and garlic; cook and stir 1 minute. Add tomatoes with juice, tomato sauce, olives and capers. Cook over medium-high heat, stirring frequently, until sauce is heated through.

3. Add sauce to pasta; mix well.   *Makes 6 to 8 servings*

Roasted Vegetables with Fettuccine

2 pounds assorted fresh vegetables*
1 envelope LIPTON® RECIPE SECRETS® Savory Herb with Garlic Soup Mix**
3 tablespoons BERTOLLI® Olive Oil
½ cup light cream, whipping or heavy cream or half-and-half
¼ cup grated Parmesan cheese
8 ounces fettuccine or linguine, cooked and drained

*Use any combination of the following, cut into 1-inch chunks: zucchini, yellow squash, red, green or yellow bell peppers, carrots, celery, onion and mushrooms.

**Also terrific with LIPTON® Recipe Secrets® Golden Onion Soup Mix.

Preheat oven to 450°F. In 13×9-inch baking or roasting pan, combine vegetables, soup mix and oil until evenly coated.

Bake uncovered, stirring once, 20 minutes or until vegetables are tender. Stir in light cream and cheese until evenly coated.

Toss with hot fettuccine. Serve, if desired, with additional grated Parmesan cheese and freshly ground black pepper.

Makes about 2 main-dish or 4 side-dish servings.

Tuscan Baked Rigatoni

1 pound Italian sausage, casings removed
1 pound rigatoni pasta, cooked, drained and kept warm
2 cups (8 ounces) shredded fontina cheese
2 tablespoons olive oil
2 fennel bulbs, thinly sliced
4 cloves garlic, minced
1 can (28 ounces) crushed tomatoes
1 cup heavy cream
1 teaspoon salt
1 teaspoon black pepper
8 cups coarsely chopped fresh spinach
1 can (15 ounces) cannellini beans, rinsed and drained
2 tablespoons pine nuts
½ cup grated Parmesan cheese

1. Preheat oven to 350°F. Spray 4-quart casserole with nonstick cooking spray. Crumble sausage into large skillet over medium-high heat. Cook and stir until no longer pink; drain. Transfer sausage to large bowl. Add pasta and fontina cheese; mix well.

2. Combine oil, fennel and garlic in same skillet. Cook and stir over medium heat 3 minutes or until fennel is tender. Add tomatoes, cream, salt and pepper; cook and stir until slightly thickened. Stir in spinach, beans and pine nuts; cook until heated through.

3. Pour sauce over pasta and sausage; toss to coat. Transfer to prepared casserole; sprinkle evenly with Parmesan cheese. Bake 30 minutes or until hot and bubbly. *Makes 6 to 8 servings*

Traditional Spaghetti Sauce

12 ounces spaghetti
1 pound mild Italian sausage
½ cup chopped onion
1 can (14.5 ounces) CONTADINA® Recipe Ready Diced Tomatoes with Roasted Garlic, undrained
1 cup chicken broth or water
1 can (6 ounces) CONTADINA Italian Paste with Italian Seasonings
1 tablespoon chopped fresh parsley

1. Cook pasta according to package directions; drain and keep warm.

2. Crumble sausage into large skillet. Cook over medium-high heat, stirring to break up sausage, 4 to 5 minutes or until no longer pink.

3. Add onion; cook 2 to 3 minutes. Drain.

4. Stir in undrained tomatoes, broth, tomato paste and parsley. Bring to a boil. Reduce heat; cook 10 to 15 minutes or until flavors are blended. Serve sauce over pasta. *Makes 4 to 6 servings*

Spaghetti with Garlic

12 ounces uncooked spaghetti
4½ teaspoons FILIPPO BERIO® Olive Oil
1 clove garlic, sliced
Salt and freshly ground black pepper
Grated Parmesan cheese

Cook pasta according to package directions until al dente (tender but still firm). Drain; transfer to large bowl. In small skillet, heat olive oil over medium heat until hot. Add garlic; cook and stir 2 to 3 minutes or until golden. Discard garlic. Pour oil over hot pasta; toss until lightly coated. Season to taste with salt and pepper. Top with cheese.

Makes 4 servings

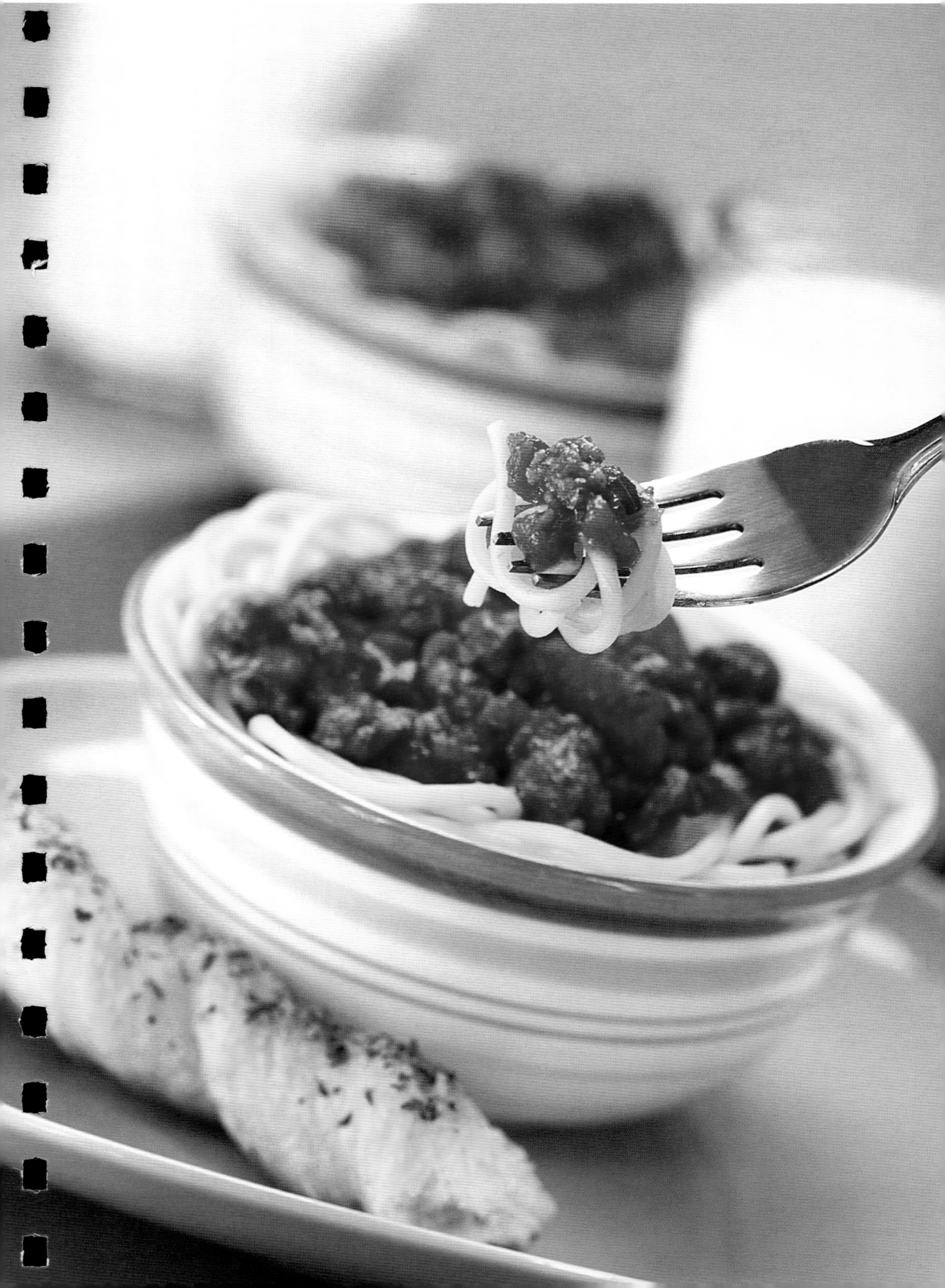

Chicken Saltimbocca

No Frying Eggplant Parmesan

Italian Pork Chop

Parmesan Turkey Breast

Effortless Entrées

No Frying Eggplant Parmesan

Prep Time: 10 minutes • **Cook Time:** 1 hour, 20 minutes

2 cups seasoned dry bread crumbs
1½ cups grated Parmesan cheese, divided
2 medium eggplants (about 2 pounds), peeled and cut into ¼-inch slices
4 eggs, beaten with 3 tablespoons water
1 jar (1 pound 10 ounces) RAGÚ® ROBUSTO!® Pasta Sauce
1½ cups shredded mozzarella cheese (about 6 ounces)

Preheat oven to 350°F. In medium bowl, combine bread crumbs and ½ cup Parmesan cheese. Dip eggplant slices in egg mixture, then bread crumb mixture. On lightly oiled baking sheets, arrange eggplant slices in single layer. Bake 25 minutes or until eggplant is golden.

In 13×9-inch baking dish, evenly spread 1 cup Ragú Pasta Sauce. Layer ½ of baked eggplant slices, then 1 cup sauce and ½ cup Parmesan cheese; repeat layers. Cover with aluminum foil and bake 45 minutes. Remove foil and sprinkle with mozzarella cheese. Bake uncovered an additional 10 minutes or until cheese is melted.   *Makes 6 servings*

Chicken Piccata

3 tablespoons all-purpose flour
½ teaspoon salt
¼ teaspoon black pepper
4 boneless skinless chicken breasts (4 ounces each)
1 tablespoon olive oil
1 tablespoon butter
2 cloves garlic, minced
¾ cup chicken broth
1 tablespoon fresh lemon juice
2 tablespoons chopped Italian parsley
1 tablespoon drained capers
Lemon slices and fresh parsley (optional)

1. Combine flour, salt and pepper in shallow pie plate. Reserve 1 tablespoon flour mixture.

2. Place chicken between sheets of plastic wrap. Using flat side of meat mallet or rolling pin, pound chicken to ½-inch thickness. Coat chicken with flour mixture, shaking off excess.

3. Heat oil and butter in large nonstick skillet over medium heat until butter is melted. Cook chicken 4 to 5 minutes per side or until no longer pink in center. Transfer to serving platter and cover loosely with foil.

4. Add garlic to same skillet; cook and stir over medium heat 1 minute. Add reserved flour mixture; cook and stir 1 minute. Add broth and lemon juice; cook 2 minutes, stirring frequently, until sauce thickens. Stir in parsley and capers; spoon sauce over chicken. Garnish with lemon slices and parsley. *Makes 4 servings*

Italian
Pork Chops

2 cups uncooked long-grain white rice
4 large pork chops (½ inch thick)
1 teaspoon basil, crushed
1 can (26 ounces) DEL MONTE® Spaghetti Sauce with
Mushrooms or Chunky Italian Herb Spaghetti Sauce
1 green bell pepper, cut into thin strips

1. Cook rice according to package directions.

2. Preheat broiler. Sprinkle meat with basil; season with salt and black pepper, if desired. Place meat on broiler pan. Broil 4 inches from heat about 6 minutes on each side or until no longer pink in center.

3. Combine sauce and green pepper in microwavable dish. Cover with plastic wrap; slit to vent. Microwave on HIGH 5 to 6 minutes or until green pepper is tender-crisp and sauce is heated through. Add meat; cover with sauce. Microwave 1 minute. Serve over hot rice.   *Makes 4 servings*

Serving Suggestion: Serve with baked potatoes and vegetables instead of rice.

Cutlets Milanese

1 package (about 1 pound) PERDUE® FIT 'N EASY®
Thin-Sliced Turkey Breast Cutlets or Chicken Breast
Salt and ground pepper to taste
½ cup Italian seasoned bread crumbs
½ cup grated Parmesan cheese
1 large egg beaten with 1 teaspoon water
2 to 3 tablespoons olive oil

Season cutlets with salt and pepper. On wax paper, combine bread crumbs and Parmesan cheese. Dip cutlets in egg mixture and roll in bread crumb mixture. In large nonstick skillet over medium-high heat, heat oil. Add cutlets and sauté 3 minutes per side or until golden brown and cooked through.   *Makes 4 servings*

Chicken Saltimbocca

¼ cup fresh basil leaves, coarsely chopped
2 tablespoons chopped fresh chives
2 teaspoons olive oil
1 clove garlic, minced
½ teaspoon dried oregano
½ teaspoon dried sage
4 boneless skinless chicken breast halves (about 4 ounces each)
2 slices (1 ounce each) smoked ham, cut in half
½ cup chicken broth
1 cup prepared pasta sauce
2 cups cooked spaghetti squash, warmed (see Tip)

1. Combine basil, chives, oil, garlic, oregano and sage in small bowl. Lightly pound chicken breasts between 2 pieces of plastic wrap with flat side of meat mallet to ½- to ¾-inch thickness. Spread one quarter of herb mixture over each chicken breast. Place 1 ham slice over herb mixture; roll up to enclose filling. Secure with toothpicks.

2. Spray medium nonstick skillet with cooking spray. Heat skillet over medium-high heat. Cook chicken breasts seam side up 2 to 3 minutes or until browned. Turn chicken; cook 2 to 3 minutes or until browned. Add broth; reduce heat to medium-low. Simmer, covered, 20 to 25 minutes or until chicken is cooked through.

3. Remove chicken to cutting board, leaving liquid in skillet. Let chicken cool 5 minutes. Add pasta sauce to skillet; cook over medium-low heat 2 to 3 minutes or until heated through, stirring occasionally.

4. Remove toothpicks from chicken and cut crosswise into slices. To serve, place spaghetti squash on serving platter or individual plates; arrange chicken slices over squash and top with pasta sauce. *Makes 4 servings*

Tip: To quickly cook spaghetti squash, cut a 2½-pound squash in half lengthwise with a sturdy sharp knife. Remove seeds from each half. Place halves cut sides down in a microwavable baking dish. Add ½ cup water, cover with plastic wrap and cook on HIGH 10 to 15 minutes or until squash is soft. Let cool 10 to 15 minutes. Scrape out squash "strands" with a fork. A 2½-pound squash yields about 4 cups cooked squash.

Classic Chicken Parmesan

6 boneless, skinless chicken breast halves, pounded thin (about 1½ pounds)
2 eggs, lightly beaten
1 cup Italian seasoned dry bread crumbs
2 tablespoons olive oil
1 jar (1 pound 10 ounces) RAGÚ® Old World Style® Pasta Sauce
1 cup shredded mozzarella cheese (about 4 ounces)

Preheat oven to 375°F. Dip chicken in eggs, then bread crumbs, coating well.

In 12-inch skillet, heat olive oil over medium-high heat and brown chicken; drain on paper towels.

In 11×7-inch baking dish, evenly spread 1 cup Ragú Pasta Sauce. Arrange chicken in dish. Top with remaining sauce. Sprinkle with mozzarella cheese and, if desired, grated Parmesan cheese. Bake uncovered 25 minutes or until chicken is thoroughly cooked.

Makes 6 servings

Recipe Tip: To pound chicken, place a boneless, skinless breast between two sheets of waxed paper. Use a rolling pin to press down and out from the center to flatten.

Shrimp Scampi

2 tablespoons olive or vegetable oil
½ cup diced onion
1 large clove garlic, minced
1 small green bell pepper, cut into strips
1 small yellow bell pepper, cut into strips
8 ounces medium shrimp, peeled, deveined
1 can (14.5 ounces) CONTADINA® Recipe Ready Diced
      Tomatoes with Italian Herbs, undrained
2 tablespoons chopped fresh parsley *or* 2 teaspoons
      dried parsley flakes
1 tablespoon lemon juice
½ teaspoon salt
      Hot cooked orzo pasta

1. Heat oil in large skillet over medium-high heat. Add onion and garlic; sauté 1 minute.

2. Add bell peppers; sauté 2 minutes. Add shrimp; cook 2 minutes or until shrimp turn pink.

3. Add undrained tomatoes, parsley, lemon juice and salt; cook 2 to 3 minutes or until heated through. Serve over hot cooked orzo pasta, if desired. *Makes 4 servings*

Tuscan Chicken with White Beans

Prep Time: 15 minutes • **Cook Time:** 35 minutes

1 large fresh fennel bulb (about ¾ pound)
1 teaspoon olive oil
1 teaspoon dried rosemary, crushed
½ teaspoon black pepper
½ pound boneless skinless chicken thighs, cut into ¾-inch
** pieces**
1 can (14½ ounces) no-salt-added stewed tomatoes
1 can (about 14 ounces) chicken broth
1 can (15 ounces) cannellini beans, rinsed and drained
** Hot pepper sauce (optional)**

1. Cut off and reserve ¼ cup chopped feathery fennel tops. Chop bulb into ½-inch pieces.

2. Heat oil in large saucepan over medium heat. Add chopped fennel bulb; cook 5 minutes, stirring occasionally.

3. Sprinkle rosemary and pepper over chicken; add to saucepan. Cook and stir 2 minutes. Add tomatoes with juice and broth; bring to a boil. Cover; simmer 10 minutes. Stir in beans; simmer, uncovered, 15 minutes or until chicken is cooked through and sauce thickens. Season to taste with hot pepper sauce. Ladle into 4 shallow bowls; top with reserved fennel tops. *Makes 4 servings*

*Quick Tip

When purchasing fennel, look for crisp, clean bulbs with bright green feathery tops. Store the whole plant (bulb and top) in a plastic bag in the refrigerator for up to five days.

Sirloin Steak Monte Carlo

2 tablespoons olive or vegetable oil
1¾ pounds sirloin steak
½ cup sliced onion
1 large clove garlic, minced
¼ cup pine nuts
1 can (14.5 ounces) CONTADINA® Italian-Style Stewed Tomatoes, undrained
2 tablespoons capers
½ teaspoon dried oregano leaves, crushed
½ teaspoon dried basil leaves, crushed
¼ teaspoon crushed red pepper flakes

1. Heat oil in large skillet over medium-high heat. Add steak; cook 4 to 5 minutes on each side for medium-rare.

2. Remove steak to platter, reserving any drippings in skillet; cover steak with foil to keep warm.

3. Add onion, garlic and pine nuts to skillet; sauté 5 minutes or until onion is tender and nuts are lightly toasted.

4. Add undrained tomatoes, capers, oregano, basil and red pepper flakes; simmer, uncovered, 5 minutes. Serve over steak.

Makes 4 to 6 servings

122 · Effortless Entrées

Chicken Tuscany

6 medium red potatoes, scrubbed and sliced ⅛ inch thick
12 ounces shiitake, cremini, chanterelle and/or button mushrooms, sliced
4 tablespoons olive oil, divided
4 tablespoons grated Parmesan cheese, divided
3 teaspoons minced garlic, divided
3 teaspoons minced fresh rosemary *or* 1½ teaspoons dried rosemary leaves, divided
   Salt and ground pepper
1 package (about 3 pounds) PERDUE® Fresh Pick of the Chicken

Preheat oven to 425°F. Pat potatoes dry with paper towels. Toss potatoes and mushrooms with 2½ tablespoons oil, 2 tablespoons cheese, 2 teaspoons garlic, 2 teaspoons rosemary, ½ teaspoon salt and ¼ teaspoon pepper. In 13×9-inch baking dish, arrange potatoes in one layer; top with remaining 2 tablespoons cheese. Bake 15 minutes or until potatoes are lightly browned; set aside.

Meanwhile, in large nonstick skillet over medium heat, heat remaining 1½ tablespoons oil. Add chicken pieces. Season lightly with salt and pepper; sprinkle with remaining 1 teaspoon rosemary and garlic. Cook chicken 5 to 6 minutes on each side or until browned. (Do not crowd pan; if necessary, brown chicken in two batches.)

Arrange chicken on top of potato mixture; drizzle with any oil from skillet and return to oven. Bake 20 to 25 minutes longer or until chicken is no longer pink in center. Serve chicken, potatoes and mushrooms with green salad, if desired. *Makes 6 servings*

Poached Seafood
Italiano

1 tablespoon olive or vegetable oil
1 large clove garlic, minced
¼ cup dry white wine or chicken broth
4 (6-ounce) salmon steaks or fillets
1 can (14.5 ounces) CONTADINA® Recipe Ready Diced
    Tomatoes with Italian Herbs, undrained
⅓ cup sliced olives (black, green or a combination)
2 tablespoons chopped fresh basil (optional)

1. Heat oil in large skillet. Add garlic; sauté 30 seconds. Add wine. Bring to a boil.

2. Add salmon; cover. Reduce heat to medium; simmer 6 minutes.

3. Add undrained tomatoes and olives; simmer 2 minutes or until salmon flakes easily when tested with fork. Sprinkle with basil just before serving, if desired.   *Makes 4 servings*

Chicken Cacciatore

2 pounds chicken parts
2 teaspoons LAWRY'S® Seasoned Salt
3 tablespoons BERTOLLI® Extra Virgin Olive Oil
1 package (1.42 ounces) LAWRY'S® Original Spaghetti Sauce
    Spices & Seasonings
1 can (14½ ounces) diced tomatoes, with juice
¼ cup dry white wine
    Cooked pasta or rice

Sprinkle chicken with Seasoned Salt. In large skillet, heat oil and brown chicken, a few pieces at a time, until golden. Remove browned pieces; drain fat. In same skillet, add Spaghetti Sauce Spices & Seasonings and tomatoes; mix well. Add chicken. Bring to a boil; reduce heat to low and cook, covered, for 10 minutes. Remove cover, add wine and cook 15 minutes longer or until chicken is thoroughly cooked. Serve over cooked pasta or rice.   *Makes 4 servings*

Parmesan Turkey Breast

½ teaspoon salt
¼ teaspoon black pepper
1 pound turkey breast, chicken breasts or veal cutlets,
cut ⅛ to ¼ inch thick
2 tablespoons butter, melted
2 cloves garlic, minced
½ cup grated Parmesan cheese
1 cup marinara sauce, warmed
2 tablespoons chopped fresh basil

1. Preheat broiler. Sprinkle salt and pepper over turkey. Place turkey in one layer in 15×10-inch jelly-roll pan.

2. Combine butter and garlic in small bowl; brush over turkey. Broil turkey 4 to 5 inches from heat source 2 minutes; turn. Sprinkle with cheese. Broil 2 to 3 minutes more or until turkey is no longer pink in center. Transfer to serving plates. To serve, spoon sauce over turkey; sprinkle with basil. *Makes 4 servings*

Variation: Preheat oven to 350°F. Sprinkle salt and pepper over turkey. Brown turkey on both sides in 1 to 2 tablespoons hot oil in medium skillet. Place browned turkey in small casserole dish or 9-inch square baking dish. Top with pasta sauce; cover dish with foil. Bake 30 minutes or until no longer pink in center. Remove from oven. Sprinkle Parmesan cheese and basil over turkey.

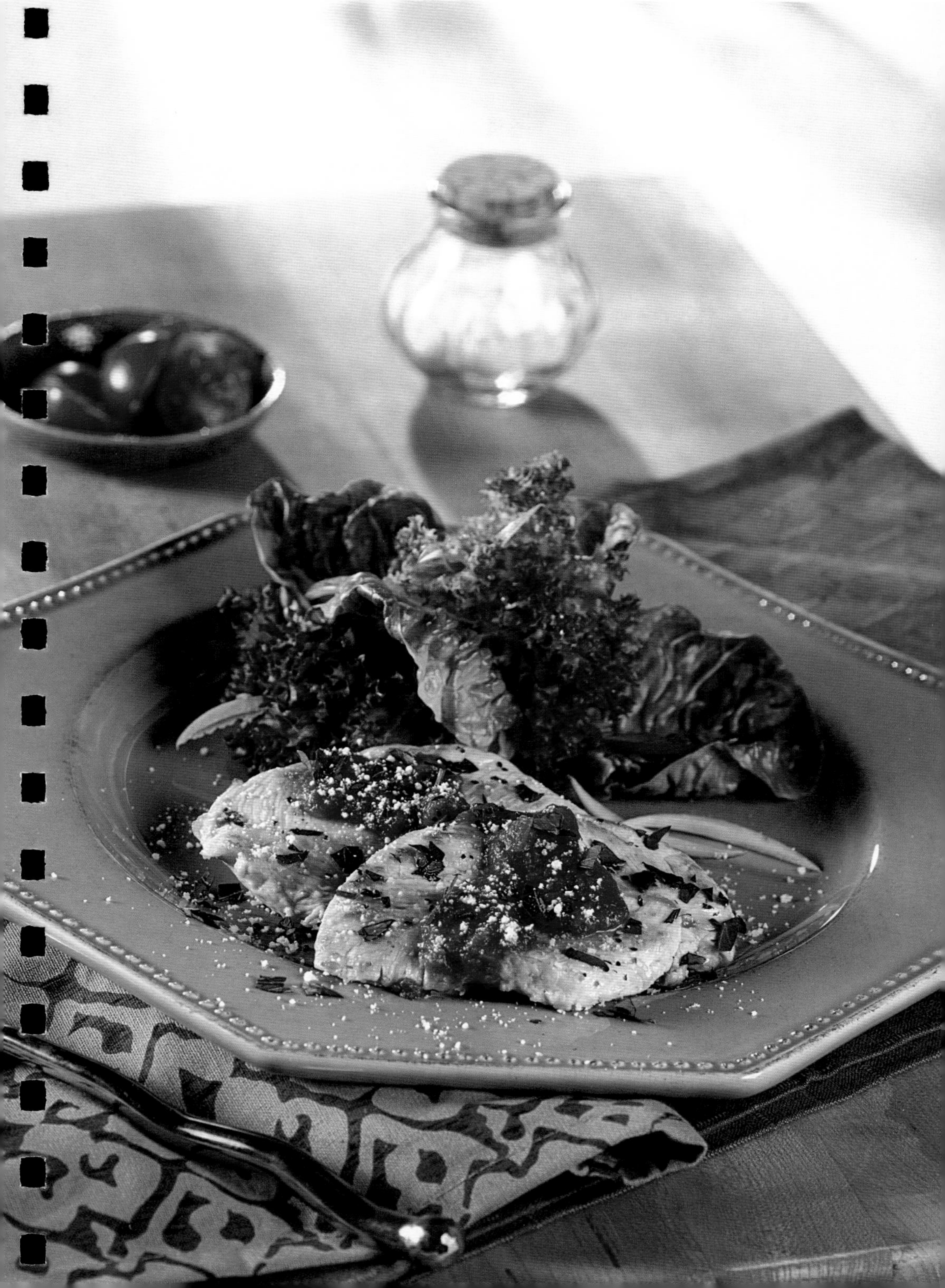

Chicken Puttanesca-Style

2 tablespoons olive oil
1 (2½- to 3-pound) chicken, cut into pieces
1 medium onion, sliced
¼ cup balsamic vinegar
1 jar (1 pound 10 ounces) RAGÚ® Old World Style® Pasta Sauce
1 cup pitted ripe olives
1 tablespoon drained capers

In 12-inch skillet, heat olive oil over medium-high heat and brown chicken. Remove chicken and set aside; drain.

In same skillet, add onion and vinegar and cook over medium heat, stirring occasionally, 3 minutes. Stir in Ragú Pasta Sauce. Return chicken to skillet and simmer covered 25 minutes or until chicken is thoroughly cooked. Stir in olives and capers; heat through. Serve, if desired, over hot cooked rice and garnish with chopped fresh parsley.

Makes 4 servings

Recipe Tip: Be sure to use the best quality balsamic vinegar you can afford. In general, the longer it's been aged, the deeper and tastier the flavor.

**Polenta with
Pasta Sauce & Vegetables**

Sautéed Garlic Potatoes

Pan-Fried Polenta with Fresh Tomato-Bean Salsa

Tomato Risotto

On the Side

Sausage & Red Pepper Risotto

4½ cups chicken broth
  8 ounces sweet Italian sausage links, removed from casing
  1 tablespoon olive oil
  1 large onion, chopped
  1 medium red bell pepper, chopped
  1 clove garlic, finely chopped
1½ cups arborio or regular rice
  ⅓ cup dry white wine or chicken broth
  ⅛ teaspoon dried oregano leaves, crushed
  1 cup RAGÚ® Light Pasta Sauce
  ¼ cup grated Parmesan cheese
  ⅛ teaspoon ground black pepper

In 2-quart saucepan, heat chicken broth; set aside.

In heavy-duty 3-quart saucepan, brown sausage over medium-high heat 4 minutes or until sausage is no longer pink; remove sausage. In same 3-quart saucepan, add olive oil and cook onion over medium heat, stirring occasionally, 3 minutes. Stir in bell pepper and garlic and cook 1 minute. Add rice and cook, stirring occasionally, 1 minute. Slowly add 1 cup hot broth, wine and oregano and cook, stirring constantly, until liquid is absorbed. Continue adding 2 cups hot broth, 1 cup at a time, stirring frequently, until liquid is absorbed.

Meanwhile, stir Ragú Pasta Sauce into remaining 1½ cups broth; heat through. Continue adding broth mixture, 1 cup at a time, stirring frequently, until rice is slightly creamy and just tender. Return sausage to saucepan and stir in cheese and black pepper. Serve immediately.

Makes 8 side-dish or 4 main-dish servings

Lemon and Fennel Marinated Vegetables

1 cup water
2 medium carrots, cut diagonally into ½-inch-thick slices
1 cup small whole fresh mushrooms
1 small red or green bell pepper, cored, seeded and cut into
     ¾-inch pieces
3 tablespoons lemon juice
1 tablespoon olive oil
1 tablespoon sugar
1 clove garlic, minced
½ teaspoon fennel seeds, crushed
½ teaspoon dried basil
¼ teaspoon black pepper

1. Bring water to a boil in small saucepan over high heat. Add carrots; return to a boil. Reduce heat to medium-low. Cover and simmer about 5 minutes or until carrots are crisp-tender. Drain and cool.

2. Place carrots, mushrooms and bell pepper in large resealable food storage bag. Combine lemon juice, oil, sugar, garlic, fennel seeds, basil and black pepper in small bowl. Pour over vegetables. Close bag securely; turn to coat. Marinate in refrigerator 8 to 24 hours, turning occasionally.

3. Drain vegetables; discard marinade. Place vegetables in serving dish.

Makes 4 servings

Pan-Fried Polenta with Fresh Tomato-Bean Salsa

2½ cups chopped plum tomatoes
1 cup canned white beans, rinsed and drained
¼ cup chopped fresh basil leaves
½ teaspoon salt
½ teaspoon black pepper
2 tablespoons olive oil
1 (16-ounce) package prepared polenta, sliced into ¼-inch-thick rounds
¼ cup grated Parmesan cheese
Additional basil leaves for garnish

1. Stir together tomatoes, beans, basil, salt and pepper. Let stand at room temperature 15 minutes to blend flavors.

2. Heat 1 tablespoon oil in medium nonstick skillet over medium-high heat. Add half of polenta slices to skillet; cook about 4 minutes or until golden brown on both sides, turning once. Remove polenta from skillet. Repeat with remaining 1 tablespoon oil and polenta slices.

3. Arrange polenta on serving plates. Top with tomato-bean mixture Sprinkle with cheese and garnish with basil leaves.   *Makes 4 servings*

*Quick Tip

Chopped fresh basil tends to bruise and discolor easily. To avoid this, stack the leaves together and roll them up cigar style. With a sharp knife, cut the leaves crosswise into strips and then make several cross cuts.

Tomato Risotto

Prep Time: 10 minutes • **Cook Time:** 30 minutes

3 tablespoons butter
1 cup sliced green onions
1½ cups uncooked Arborio rice or medium-grain white rice
1 can (14.5 ounces) BUTTERBALL® Chicken Broth
1 can (14.5 ounces) HUNT'S® Diced Tomatoes with Green Pepper, Celery and Onions, undrained
¾ cup grated Parmesan cheese
¼ teaspoon salt
¼ teaspoon ground black pepper

MELT butter in a large skillet over medium heat; add green onions and sauté for about 1 minute. Stir in rice; cook an additional 2 minutes.

ADD broth and tomatoes. Bring to a boil, cover and reduce heat to low; simmer for 20 minutes.

SIMMER, uncovered, 5 minutes, stirring occasionally. Remove from heat; blend in cheese. Season with salt and pepper. *Makes 6 servings*

BelGioioso® Parmesan Polenta

Nonstick vegetable oil spray
4 cups canned vegetable broth
1½ cups yellow cornmeal
¾ cup grated BELGIOIOSO® Parmesan Cheese (about 2 ounces)

Preheat oven to 375°F. Spray 8×8×2-inch glass baking dish with vegetable oil spray. Bring vegetable broth to a boil in medium heavy saucepan over medium heat. Gradually whisk in cornmeal. Continue to whisk until mixture is very thick, about 3 minutes. Mix in BelGioioso Parmesan Cheese and pour mixture into prepared dish. Bake polenta until top begins to brown, about 30 minutes. Serve hot.

Makes 4 to 6 servings

Eggplant Italiano

2 tablespoons olive oil, divided
2 medium onions, thinly sliced
2 ribs celery, cut into 1-inch pieces
1¼ pounds eggplant, cut into 1-inch cubes
1 can (16 ounces) diced tomatoes, drained
½ cup pitted ripe olives, cut crosswise in half
2 tablespoons balsamic vinegar
1 tablespoon sugar
1 tablespoon capers, drained
1 teaspoon dried oregano or basil leaves
   Salt and black pepper to taste

1. Heat large skillet over medium-high heat 1 minute or until hot. Drizzle 1 tablespoon oil into skillet and heat 30 seconds. Add onions and celery; cook and stir about 2 minutes or until tender. Move onions and celery to side of skillet. Reduce heat to medium.

2. Add remaining 1 tablespoon oil to bottom of skillet and heat 30 seconds. Add eggplant; cook and stir about 4 minutes or until tender. Add tomatoes; mix well. Cover and cook 10 minutes.

3. Stir olives, vinegar, sugar, capers and oregano into eggplant mixture. Season with salt and pepper.   *Makes 6 servings*

Sautéed Garlic Potatoes

2 pounds boiling potatoes, peeled and cut into 1-inch pieces
3 tablespoons FILIPPO BERIO® Olive Oil
6 cloves garlic, unpeeled
1 tablespoon lemon juice
1 tablespoon chopped fresh chives
1 tablespoon chopped fresh parsley
Salt and freshly ground black pepper

Place potatoes in large colander; rinse under cold running water. Drain well; pat dry. In large nonstick skillet, heat olive oil over medium heat until hot. Add potatoes in single layer. Cook, stirring and turning frequently, 10 minutes or until golden brown. Add garlic. Cover; reduce heat to low and cook very gently, shaking pan and stirring mixture occasionally, 15 to 20 minutes or until potatoes are tender when pierced with fork. Remove garlic; remove and discard skins. In small bowl, crush garlic; stir in lemon juice. Add to potatoes; mix well. Cook 1 to 2 minutes or until heated through. Transfer to serving dish; sprinkle with chives and parsley. Season to taste with salt and pepper. *Makes 4 servings*

Broccoli Italian Style

1¼ pounds broccoli
2 tablespoons lemon juice
1 teaspoon olive oil
1 clove garlic, minced
1 teaspoon chopped fresh parsley
Dash black pepper

Trim broccoli, discarding tough part of stems. Cut broccoli into florets with 2-inch stems. Peel remaining broccoli stems; cut into ½-inch-thick slices. Bring 1 quart water to a boil in large saucepan. Add broccoli; return to a boil. Cook, uncovered, 3 to 5 minutes over medium-high heat or until broccoli is fork-tender. Drain and transfer to serving dish.

Combine lemon juice, oil, garlic, parsley and pepper. Pour over broccoli, turning to coat. Let stand, covered, 1 to 2 hours. *Makes 4 servings*

Zucchini-Tomato Bake

1 pound eggplant, coarsely chopped
2 cups zucchini slices
2 cups mushroom slices
2 teaspoons olive oil
½ cup chopped onion
½ cup chopped fresh fennel (optional)
2 cloves garlic, minced
1 can (14½ ounces) no-salt-added whole tomatoes, undrained
1 tablespoon no-salt-added tomato paste
2 teaspoons dried basil
1 teaspoon sugar

1. Preheat oven to 400°F. Spray 3 sheets (18×12 inches) heavy-duty foil with nonstick cooking spray. Divide eggplant, zucchini and mushrooms into 3 portions. Arrange each portion on foil sheet.

2. Heat oil in small skillet over medium heat. Add onion, fennel and garlic. Cook and stir 3 to 4 minutes or until onion is tender. Add tomatoes with juice, tomato paste, basil and sugar. Cook and stir about 4 minutes or until sauce thickens.

3. Pour sauce over eggplant mixture. Double-fold sides and ends of foil to seal packets, leaving head space for heat circulation. Place on baking sheet.

4. Bake 30 minutes. Remove from oven. Carefully open one end of each packet to allow steam to escape. Open and transfer contents to serving dish. Garnish, if desired. *Makes 6 servings*

Baked Risotto with Asparagus, Spinach & Parmesan

1 tablespoon olive oil
1 cup finely chopped onion
1 cup arborio rice
8 cups (8 to 10 ounces) spinach leaves, torn into pieces
2 cups chicken broth
¼ teaspoon salt
¼ teaspoon ground nutmeg
½ cup grated Parmesan cheese, divided
1½ cups diagonally sliced asparagus

1. Preheat oven to 400°F. Spray 13×9-inch baking dish with nonstick cooking spray.

2. Heat olive oil in large skillet over medium-high heat. Add onion; cook and stir 4 minutes or until tender. Add rice; stir to coat with oil.

3. Stir in spinach, a handful at a time, adding more as it wilts. Add broth, salt and nutmeg. Reduce heat and simmer 7 minutes. Stir in ¼ cup cheese.

4. Transfer to prepared baking dish. Cover tightly and bake 15 minutes.

5. Remove from oven and stir in asparagus; sprinkle with remaining ¼ cup cheese. Cover and bake 15 minutes more or until liquid is absorbed. *Makes 8 to 10 side-dish servings*

Italian Vegetables with Garlic Butter Rice

Prep Time: 5 minutes • **Cook Time:** 15 minutes

- **1 yellow squash, sliced**
- **1 zucchini, sliced**
- **1 cup diced red bell pepper**
- **1 cup sliced eggplant**
- **⅓ cup balsamic vinaigrette**
- **1 tablespoon chopped fresh rosemary**
- **1 package UNCLE BEN'S FLAVORFUL™ Garlic & Butter Rice**

PREP: In large bowl, combine vegetables, vinaigrette and rosemary; set aside 15 minutes.

COOK: Meanwhile, prepare rice according to package directions; set aside. Sauté vegetables in marinade until crisp-tender.

SERVE: Serve vegetable mixture over rice.

CHILL: Refrigerate leftovers immediately. *Makes 4 servings*

Peas Florentine Style

- **2 (10-ounce) packages frozen peas**
- **¼ cup FILIPPO BERIO® Olive Oil**
- **4 ounces Canadian bacon, cubed**
- **1 clove garlic, minced**
- **1 tablespoon chopped fresh Italian parsley**
- **1 teaspoon sugar**
- **Salt**

Place peas in large colander or strainer; run under hot water until slightly thawed. Drain well. In medium skillet, heat olive oil over medium heat until hot. Add bacon and garlic; cook and stir 2 to 3 minutes or until garlic turns golden. Add peas and parsley; cook and stir over high heat 5 to 7 minutes or until heated through. Drain well. Stir in sugar; season to taste with salt. *Makes 5 servings*

Polenta with Pasta Sauce & Vegetables

Prep Time: 5 minutes • **Cook Time:** 15 minutes

1 can (about 14 ounces) reduced-sodium chicken broth
1½ cups water
1 cup yellow cornmeal
1 tablespoon olive oil
12 ounces assorted cut-up vegetables, such as broccoli florets, bell peppers, red onions, zucchini and thin carrot strips
2 teaspoons minced garlic
2 cups prepared tomato-basil pasta sauce
½ cup grated Asiago cheese
¼ cup chopped fresh basil (optional)

1. To prepare polenta, whisk together broth, water and cornmeal in large microwavable bowl. Cover with waxed paper; microwave on HIGH 5 minutes. Whisk well and microwave on HIGH 4 to 5 minutes more or until polenta is very thick. Whisk again; cover and keep warm.

2. Meanwhile, heat oil in large deep nonstick skillet over medium heat. Add vegetables and garlic; cook and stir 5 minutes. Add pasta sauce; reduce heat, cover and simmer 5 to 8 minutes or until vegetables are tender.

3. Spoon polenta onto serving plates; top with pasta sauce mixture. Sprinkle with cheese and basil. *Makes 4 servings*

Peasant Risotto

1 tablespoon olive oil
3 ounces chopped ham
2 cloves garlic, minced
1 cup arborio or white short-grain rice
1 can (15 ounces) Great Northern beans, rinsed and drained
¼ cup chopped green onions
½ teaspoon dried sage leaves
2 cans (14 ounces each) reduced-sodium chicken broth, heated
1½ cups Swiss chard, rinsed, stemmed and shredded
¼ cup freshly grated Parmesan cheese

1. Heat oil in large saucepan over medium heat. Add ham and garlic; cook and stir until garlic is browned. Add rice, beans, green onions and sage; mix well. Add warm broth; bring to a boil. Reduce heat to low. Cook about 25 minutes or until rice is creamy, stirring frequently.

2. Add Swiss chard and Parmesan; mix well. Cover; remove from heat. Let stand, covered, 2 minutes or until Swiss chard is wilted. Serve immediately. *Makes 4 servings*

The publisher would like to thank the companies and organizations listed below for the use of their recipes and photographs in this publication.

Bays English Muffin Corporation

BelGioioso® Cheese, Inc.

ConAgra Foods®

Crisco is a registered trademark of The J.M. Smucker Company

Del Monte Corporation

Filippo Berio® Olive Oil

The Golden Grain Company®

The Hidden Valley® Food Products Company

Hillshire Farm®

Hormel Foods, LLC

Lawry's® Foods

MASTERFOODS USA

McIlhenny Company (TABASCO® brand Pepper Sauce)

Perdue Farms Incorporated

Reckitt Benckiser Inc.

Sargento® Foods Inc.

Sonoma® Dried Tomatoes

Unilever Foods North America

VOLUME MEASUREMENTS (dry)

$1/8$ teaspoon = 0.5 mL
$1/4$ teaspoon = 1 mL
$1/2$ teaspoon = 2 mL
$3/4$ teaspoon = 4 mL
1 teaspoon = 5 mL
1 tablespoon = 15 mL
2 tablespoons = 30 mL
$1/4$ cup = 60 mL
$1/3$ cup = 75 mL
$1/2$ cup = 125 mL
$2/3$ cup = 150 mL
$3/4$ cup = 175 mL
1 cup = 250 mL
2 cups = 1 pint = 500 mL
3 cups = 750 mL
4 cups = 1 quart = 1 L

VOLUME MEASUREMENTS (fluid)

1 fluid ounce (2 tablespoons) = 30 mL
4 fluid ounces ($1/2$ cup) = 125 mL
8 fluid ounces (1 cup) = 250 mL
12 fluid ounces ($1 1/2$ cups) = 375 mL
16 fluid ounces (2 cups) = 500 mL

WEIGHTS (mass)

$1/2$ ounce = 15 g
1 ounce = 30 g
3 ounces = 90 g
4 ounces = 120 g
8 ounces = 225 g
10 ounces = 285 g
12 ounces = 360 g
16 ounces = 1 pound = 450 g

DIMENSIONS

$1/16$ inch = 2 mm
$1/8$ inch = 3 mm
$1/4$ inch = 6 mm
$1/2$ inch = 1.5 cm
$3/4$ inch = 2 cm
1 inch = 2.5 cm

OVEN TEMPERATURES

250°F = 120°C
275°F = 140°C
300°F = 150°C
325°F = 160°C
350°F = 180°C
375°F = 190°C
400°F = 200°C
425°F = 220°C
450°F = 230°C

BAKING PAN SIZES

Utensil	Size in Inches/Quarts	Metric Volume	Size in Centimeters
Baking or Cake Pan (square or rectangular)	$8 \times 8 \times 2$	2 L	$20 \times 20 \times 5$
	$9 \times 9 \times 2$	2.5 L	$23 \times 23 \times 5$
	$12 \times 8 \times 2$	3 L	$30 \times 20 \times 5$
	$13 \times 9 \times 2$	3.5 L	$33 \times 23 \times 5$
Loaf Pan	$8 \times 4 \times 3$	1.5 L	$20 \times 10 \times 7$
	$9 \times 5 \times 3$	2 L	$23 \times 13 \times 7$
Round Layer Cake Pan	$8 \times 1 1/2$	1.2 L	20×4
	$9 \times 1 1/2$	1.5 L	23×4
Pie Plate	$8 \times 1 1/4$	750 mL	20×3
	$9 \times 1 1/4$	1 L	23×3
Baking Dish or Casserole	1 quart	1 L	—
	$1 1/2$ quart	1.5 L	—
	2 quart	2 L	—